Bristol & Bath, Somerset and Gloucestershire

NIGEL VILE

COUNTRYSIDE BOOKS
NEWBURY BERKSHIRE

First published 2005
© Nigel Vile, 2005

COUNTRYSIDE BOOKS
3 Catherine Road
Newbury, Berkshire

To view our complete range of books,
please visit us at
www.countrysidebooks.co.uk

ISBN 1 85306 896 9

Photographs and maps by the author

Designed by Peter Davies, Nautilus Design
Produced through MRM Associates Ltd., Reading
Typeset by Techniset Typesetters, Newton-le-Willows
Printed by Woolnough Bookbinding Ltd., Irthlingborough

Contents

INTRODUCTION

WALKS IN THE BRISTOL & BATH REGION

1. **Kewstoke:** The New Inn (7 miles) — 8
2. **Rowberrow:** The Swan Inn (6 miles) — 12
3. **Priddy:** The New Inn (6 miles) — 15
4. **Wookey Hole:** The Wookey Hole Inn (5 miles) — 18
5. **Litton:** The King's Arms (3½ miles) — 21
6. **Mells:** The Talbot Inn (5 miles) — 24
7. **Wellow:** The Fox & Badger (6 miles) — 27
8. **Freshford:** The Inn at Freshford (6 miles) — 30
9. **Monkton Farleigh:** The King's Arms (5 miles) — 33
10. **Kelston:** The Old Crown Inn (4 miles) — 36
11. **Marshfield:** The Catherine Wheel (6 miles) — 39
12. **Castle Combe:** The White Hart (4 miles) — 42
13. **Old Sodbury:** The Dog Inn (5 miles) — 45
14. **Littleton upon Severn:** The White Hart (5 miles) — 48
15. **Hawkesbury Upton:** The Beaufort Arms (4 miles) — 51

WALKS IN SOMERSET

16. **Exford:** The White Horse Inn (5 miles) — 54
17. **Wheddon Cross:** The Rest & Be Thankful Inn (5 miles) — 57
18. **Winsford:** The Royal Oak Inn (4 miles) — 60
19. **Kilve:** The Hood Arms (6 miles) — 63
20. **Triscombe:** The Blue Ball Inn (5 miles) — 66
21. **Combwich:** The Anchor Inn (7 miles) — 69
22. **Creech St Michael:** The Riverside Tavern (5 miles) — 72
23. **Westonzoyland:** The Sedgemoor Inn (6 miles) — 75
24. **Long Sutton:** The Devonshire Angel (6 miles) — 78
25. **Montacute:** The King's Arms Inn (5 miles) — 81
26. **South Cadbury:** The Red Lion (6 miles) — 84
27. **Bruton:** The Blue Ball Hotel (4 miles) — 87

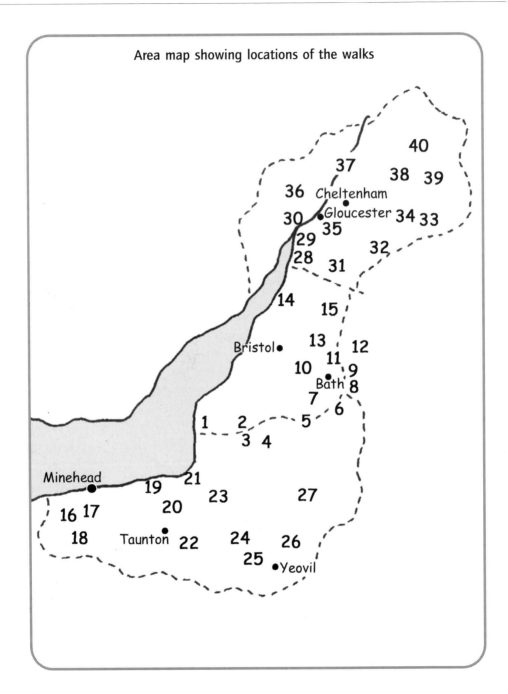

Area map showing locations of the walks

Contents

WALKS IN GLOUCESTERSHIRE

28. Ham: The Salutation (6 miles) — 90

29. Purton: The Berkeley Arms (4½ miles) — 93

30. Awre: The Red Hart (3½ miles) — 96

31. Uley: The Old Crown Inn (5 miles) — 99

32. Sapperton: The Bell Inn (3½ miles) — 102

33. Coln St Aldwyns: The New Inn (6½ miles) — 105

34. Chedworth: The Seven Tuns (4½ miles) — 108

35. Painswick: The Falcon Inn (5 miles) — 111

36. Glasshouse: The Glasshouse Inn (4½ miles) — 114

37. Tirley: The Haw Bridge Inn (5 miles) — 117

38. Brockhampton: The Craven Arms (3 miles) — 120

39. Bourton-on-the-Water: The Old Manse Hotel (5 miles) — 123

40. Stanton: The Mount Inn (5 miles) — 126

PUBLISHER'S NOTE

We hope that you obtain considerable enjoyment from this book; great care has been taken in its preparation. Although at the time of publication all routes followed public rights of way or permitted paths, diversion orders can be made and permissions withdrawn.

We cannot, of course, be held responsible for such diversion orders and any inaccuracies in the text which result from these or any other changes to the routes nor for any damage which might result from walkers trespassing on private property. We are anxious though that all details covering the walks are kept up to date and would therefore welcome information from readers which would be relevant to future editions.

The simple sketch maps that accompany the walks in this book are based on notes made by the author whilst checking out the routes on the ground. However, for the benefit of a proper map, we do recommend that you purchase the relevant Ordnance Survey sheet covering your walk. The Ordnance Survey maps are widely available, especially through booksellers and local newsagents.

Introduction

What better way to spend a leisurely few hours than to drive out to the countryside, stretch your legs and then visit a traditional pub for a delicious meal or snack and a glass of beer or wine. The 40 circular walks in this book allow you to do just that. Each route, starting and finishing at – or very close to – a recommended pub, takes you through some of the finest scenery in either Gloucestershire or Somerset, or in the area around Bath and Bristol. This was formerly the county of Avon, which has now been divided up into four unitary authorities – Bristol, North Somerset, South Gloucestershire and Bath & North East Somerset.

Gloucestershire – now a rival to Berkshire as the 'Royal County' on account of its large number of royal residences – offers a variety of walking opportunities for the visitor. Firstly there are the Cotswolds, that much-loved limestone region stretching from Chipping Campden in a southerly direction towards Bath. Here is a landscape of drystone walls and picture postcard villages, sparkling rivers and rolling wolds. It is little wonder that this delightful part of England appears on many a calendar or jigsaw puzzle. Below the Cotswolds lies the Severn Vale, an area where small family farms and traditional farming practices still hold sway. Meadows and country lanes stretch away to the great river, on its way from the mountains of Mid Wales to the Bristol Channel. Cast your eye across the river and you will see the wooded slopes and hills of the Forest of Dean, a remote and isolated corner of the county with a real off-the-beaten track feel.

And then there is Somerset – Gloucestershire's great rival on the cricket field as well as a great rival in terms of what it can offer the visitor. Here we find Exmoor, a much-loved National Park, whose heather and bracken clad moors are home to red deer and the famous Exmoor ponies. Then there are the Quantock Hills and the Mendips, where the upland rises to well over 1,000 feet above sea level. By way of complete contrast there are the Somerset Levels, a flat, low-lying landscape that was in former times little more than bog and marsh. This horizontal landscape is now home to a rich array of moisture-loving flora and fauna, a veritable naturalist's paradise. The whole area is bounded by the Bristol Channel coast, whose crumbling cliffs and sea-views attract visitors from far and near.

In between is the area around Bath and Bristol, formerly subsumed by these two historic counties but now a collection of political entities in their own right. Many a local resident harks back to the former days, with campaigns to 'return Bath to Somerset' or 'Chipping Sodbury to Gloucestershire' often attracting correspondence in the local media. Although very much an urban and suburban area, there are plenty of fine walking opportunities around these two great cities. The Southern Cotswolds and the Northern Mendips spill over into this region, for example, whilst to the west lie the mud flats and tidal expanses of the Severn Estuary. Beyond Bath there is the spectacular Avon Valley, whose steep wooded slopes run through to the delightful town of Bradford-on-Avon.

Admiring the view over the Somerset Levels

These 40 circular routes are between 3 and 7 miles in length. You will usually be able to park at the pub whilst doing the walk as long as you intend to call in for some refreshment. It is only common courtesy, however, to seek the landlord's permission first, permission which may not be forthcoming on busy weekends and bank holidays when parking is at a premium. In such cases, alternative parking options nearby have been described. Each walk is accompanied by a sketch map, indicating the route to be followed. However, I would always recommend carrying the relevant OS Explorer or Outdoor Leisure map as well – these are as vital a part of the walker's kit as sturdy boots and a rucksack, and the appropriate sheet number is given at the start of each chapter.

To make your day out complete, don't forget to carry a snack and drink in that trustworthy rucksack, as well as a decent set of waterproofs. Despite occasional belief to the contrary, the authors of walking guidebooks cannot guarantee their readers sunny weather! And remember that rain creates muddy paths, and no publican wants a trail of mud through the lounge or public bar – do attempt some form of wash and brush-up before entering these fine hostelries.

It just remains for me to wish you many happy hours of pleasure in following these pub walks.

Nigel Vile

Kewstoke

The New Inn

With its Grand Pier and arcades, Weston-super-Mare is the archetypal English seaside resort. Head a couple of miles north along the coast, however, and the scene is altogether different. Sand Bay is as remote and desolate as Weston is glitzy and commercialised, whilst the rocky headland at Sand Point and Middle Hope is as rugged and spectacular as any stretch of coast along the Bristol Channel. The views from the coastal path are never less than impressive, ranging from the Severn Crossings above Avonmouth

to the Welsh coast and the distant Black Mountains. Woodspring Priory, an Augustinian house of the rare Victorine rule, is but another of the highlights along the way on this truly impressive coastal excursion.

The **New Inn** at Kewstoke is a good old-fashioned local hostelry that has made few concessions to ephemeral contemporary tastes. Around its lounge and public bar areas lie mementoes of the local darts and cribbage teams based in the pub, whilst historic prints and photos show the New Inn in years gone by. The traditional no-frills food available includes ploughman's and sandwiches, salads and jacket potatoes, as well as fish dishes, curries, chilli and chicken options. Unusually for this part of the country, beers from the St Austell Brewery in Cornwall are available, including Tribute pale brown ale.

Opening times are 12 noon to 3 pm and 6 pm to 11 pm every day.

Telephone: 01934 622766.

Distance: 7 miles

OS Explorer 153 Weston-super-Mare GR 336634

An extended stroll along the Bristol Channel coast, with only the occasional gentle climb along the way

Starting point: The car park at the New Inn, Kewstoke – but ask the landlord's permission to leave your car while you are walking.

How to get there: Leave the M5 at junction 21 and head into Weston. Almost immediately, at the first road junction, follow the signs for Sand Bay. In 2½ miles, at a junction where the right turn is to Sand Bay, keep left towards Kewstoke. The New Inn is on the right-hand side of the road in approximately ½ mile. As an alternative to using the inn's car park, there is roadside parking opposite. On the road above the inn, Kewstoke Chapel's car park is open to the public from Monday to Friday.

The Walk

1 Leave the car park, turn right and follow the road uphill to a road junction.

Turn left along Kewstoke Road into Kewstoke. Follow this road for ¾ mile to a left turn – Norton Lane – and walk down Norton Lane for 350 yards to a

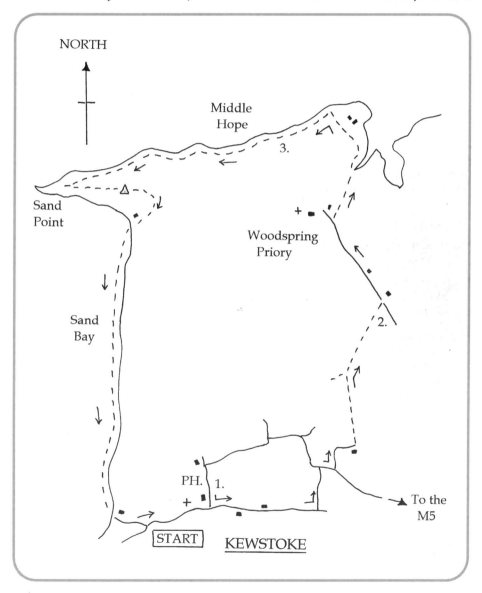

NORTH

Middle Hope

3.

Sand Point

Woodspring Priory

Sand Bay

2.

PH. 1.

To the M5

START   KEWSTOKE

Woodspring Priory, founded in 1210

junction. Turn right – signposted to Weston and Bristol – and, in 150 yards, left along an unmarked lane immediately before Norton Court Farm. Follow this lane – it soon bears right – around to Myrtle Farm. Beyond the farm on the right, continue along an unmetalled track that shortly bears left around the side of a stable block. Continue along this track for 600 yards to a junction, turn right and continue for ¼ mile until the track ends at a gate and open field. Follow the left edge of the field ahead, and continue around the end field boundary before passing through a gate on the left into the next field. Bear right and cross this field to another gate and lane.

2 Turn left and follow this lane for ½ mile to the parking area for Woodspring Priory. Detour ahead if you wish to visit the Priory. For the main walk, however, follow a track on the right before some farm buildings to some steps and the banks of a river estuary. Turn left and follow the bank of this inlet. Where the clear path ends, turn left up a hillside to a gate and open hilltop. Beyond this gate, turn right and follow the line of a fence on the right to a drive leading to an MOD property. Pass through a gap in the stone wall opposite, before walking towards the Bristol Channel, keeping the fence surrounding the MOD property to the right. On reaching the edge of the hilltop above the Channel, turn left and follow a line of gorse bushes that line the edge of the hilltop. In 400 yards, follow a track through these gorse bushes down to the start of a bay called Middle Hope.

❸ Follow the path above the bay around to a wall, cross the ladder stile and continue along the path immediately above the bay. On the far side of this pebble-strewn inlet, keep right at a fork and follow the clifftop path above the Channel for ½ mile until the path ends at a stile. Continue uphill towards Sand Point – the path is fairly rough and uneven – to reach a junction with the ridge-top path. Turn left and follow this ridge-top path for ¼ mile to reach the trig point high on this rocky promontory. Follow the right edge of the grassy area alongside the trig point to a path, and drop downhill to reach the end of the coast road below Sand Point. Turn right to a wall behind a toilet block, drop down onto the foreshore and walk the whole length of Sand Bay – almost 1½ miles. At the end of the beach, follow the road back up to Kewstoke and the New Inn.

Date walk completed:

15 | 2 | 10 .

Places of Interest

Woodspring Priory was founded in 1210, perhaps as an expiatory gesture, by William de Courtenay, grandson of Reginald FitzUrse who, with other West Country men, murdered Thomas à Becket. It was an Augustinian house of the rare Victorine rule, and had St Thomas the Martyr as a patron saint. Although small, it flourished in the 15th century, when the tower and nave of the church, the infirmary and a great barn were built of a beautiful golden stone. The north aisle was unfinished when, in 1536, the Priory was suppressed and the church, most unusually, turned into a dwelling, a chimneystack built up through the roof of the nave. Woodspring Priory is open from 9 am until 7 pm in the summer, and from 9 am until dusk in the winter months. It is owned and administered by the Landmark Trust who can be contacted on 01628 825925.

Weston-super-Mare – with its Grand Pier and Old Pier, its promenade and Winter Gardens – lies just a mile or two south of Sand Bay. The **North Somerset Museum** is a particular highlight of this Victorian resort. Its displays document the history and development of the town, from a diminutive fishing port to its emergence as one of the country's leading seaside venues due to the growth of the railway network. Telephone 01934 621028 for further information.

Rowberrow

The Swan Inn

A n energetic walk on the Mendip Hills. The scenery throughout is magnificent, and includes the limestone cliffs and pot-holes of Burrington, the extensive views from the ramparts of Dolebury Hillfort, the wooded slopes of Rowberrow Bottom that belie the area's former status as a mining centre and the bracken-and-heather clad slopes of Blackdown. In Burrington Combe, a cleft in a steep rock face gave shelter to the Reverend Augustus Toplady during a storm in 1762. Whilst seeking respite from the elements, he was inspired to write the well-known hymn *Rock of Ages*, just another of the surprises along the way on this fine walk. To enjoy the extensive views, be sure to wait until high pressure is firmly in place before tackling this upland excursion.

The **Swan Inn** is a traditional hostelry, with a welcoming atmosphere for both locals and visitors alike. Internally, there are two main bar areas, both furnished in a tasteful and comfortable manner. The flagstone floors have largely been hidden beneath carpeting, but a number of original features remain. These include an abundance of black beams and some exposed stonework. Whether your appetite is limited to sandwiches or jacket potatoes, or can encompass steak and kidney pudding or large steaks, the Swan offers a complete range of hearty pub food. To accompany your meal, try a glass of Butcombe Bitter or Thatcher's Scrumpy, both brewed in the area.

Opening times are 12 noon to 3 pm and 5.30 pm to 11 pm on Monday to Friday; 12 noon to 11 pm on Saturday; 12 noon to 10.30 pm on Sunday.

Telephone: 01934 852371.

Distance: *6 miles*

OS Explorer 141 Cheddar Gorge and Mendip Hills West
GR 451583

Wooded valleys and open exposed hilltops, with several climbs along the way

Starting point: The Swan Inn at Rowberrow, but ask permission from the landlord before using the inn's car park while you walk.

How to get there: Leave the A38 just south of Churchill on its way south towards Axbridge, and follow an unclassified road into Rowberrow. The Swan Inn is ¼ mile on from the village church.

The Walk

1 Follow School Lane as it runs along the side of the Swan Inn before bearing right and dropping downhill into Rowberrow Warren. Continue along what becomes an unmetalled track running through the valley bottom, passing a number of isolated properties along the way, until in ½ mile you reach a fenced enclosure containing a waterboard installation. Turn left, crossing the stream that runs through this wooded valley, before bearing left uphill along a track signposted to Blackdown. Follow the main woodland track, ignoring all side turns, for ¾ mile until the path emerges beyond a gateway onto the open hilltop of Blackdown.

2 Follow the main path ahead – ignoring a path forking off to the left – across the hilltop. In ¼ mile, this path crosses a broad grassy ride. In another 200 yards,

turn left along a less well-defined path that shortly drops downhill whilst bordering the western edge of a valley containing West Twin Brook. Drop downhill for ½ mile before forking right onto a minor side path that heads down into a clearly visible wooded combe. Follow this path down through the combe – it could resemble a riverbed following heavy rainfall! – to reach the B3134. Turn left and follow the path in the woodland bordering the main road down into Burrington Combe, passing Aveline's Hole and the Rock of Ages along the way.

3 Walk down past the Burrington Freehouse and, opposite the garden centre, fork left onto an overgrown track that leads to a cottage. Immediately before this cottage, turn left and follow a path uphill to reach a quiet back lane. Turn left and, in 100 yards, right along a signposted footpath into Mendip Lodge

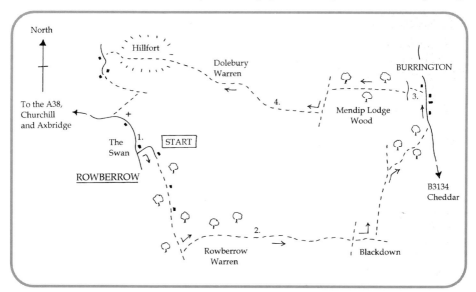

Wood. In ¾ mile, pass to the right of an old limekiln to reach a clearing where the path forks. Keep right to another old building, pass to the left of this and continue to a wooden barrier and a track. Turn left and continue uphill for ¼ mile to a stile and gate on the right and a National Trust 'Dolebury Warren' sign. Cross this stile, and head across the field ahead towards an area of scrubland.

4 On reaching the corner of this scrub, cross a stile on the right, bear left and head uphill through the trees and bushes. Follow the main path, shortly passing an area of conifers on the left, to reach a gate and stile. Continue following the ridge path ahead to reach Dolebury Hillfort. Descend the far side of the hillfort before following a winding path downhill through woodland to reach a gate and access road to a

Rowberry church, passed on the walk

number of properties. Turn left along this lane, passing some cottages, to reach another road in 150 yards. Follow this lane to the left for 150 yards to a gateway, before continuing along a muddy track through Dolebury Bottom for 250 yards. At this point, turn sharply right to follow an occasionally overgrown path up out of the valley bottom to reach a lane. Turn left, pass Rowberrow church and continue for ¼ mile back to the Swan Inn.

Place of Interest

At nearby **Axbridge**, in the corner of the square that was originally used for the cruel sport of bull baiting during the 1600s, stands a Tudor merchant's house. This timber-framed structure dating from 1500 was extensively restored in 1971. The building, known as **King John's Hunting Lodge**, is a National Trust property and is run as a museum of local history and archaeology. It is open to the public from April through to September. Telephone 01934 732012 for details.

Date walk completed:

....

stack of hurdles awaits the annual sheep fair. South of Priddy lies Deer Leap, a spectacular viewpoint whose outlook extends as far as Exmoor and the Bristol Channel, whilst above the village is North Hill, the site of a collection of mysterious round barrows. You will also pass through Priddy Minery, a site of lead excavation whose 'gruffy ground' also houses a number of former washing pools that are now fine habitats for the dragonfly.

The village of Priddy – standing at over 800 feet above sea level – is often called the capital of the Mendips. Its grey-walled community is grouped around the green, where a

The **New Inn**, overlooking Priddy's picturesque village green, is a centuries old cottage-style hostelry that has been extended in recent years to offer accommodation as well as sustenance. Internally, there are both public and lounge bars, the lounge boasting a fine log fire in winter. Visitors will also find a conservatory area as well as a garden for those warm summer days. The delicious home-cooked food ranges from rolls, sandwiches and salads through to fish, steak and chicken dishes. To accompany your meal, a glass of Wadworth 6X or the locally brewed Butcombe Bitter is highly recommended.

Distance: *6 miles*

OS Explorer 141 Cheddar Gorge and Mendip Hills West
GR 528509

An energetic walk that includes a climb onto the 1,000 foot summit of North Hill

Starting point: Alongside the New Inn at Priddy.

How to get there: Leave the main A39 at Green Ore, 4 miles north of Wells, and head in a westerly direction along the B3135 towards Cheddar. In 5 miles, follow the unclassified road signposted to Priddy. When you reach the centre of the village, the New Inn is clearly visible fronting onto the green. Park on the gravelled parking area by the public telephone box.

Opening times are 12 noon to 3 pm and 6 pm to 11 pm on Sunday to Thursday, and from 11.30 am on Friday and Saturday. Food is served from 12 noon to 2 pm and 7 pm to 9 pm.

Telephone: 01749 676465.

The Walk

1 Follow the lane across the green – passing in front of the New Inn – to reach a minor crossroads. Turn left into a cul-de-sac and, where this lane ends by a property called Trails End, cross the stile ahead before walking across three fields, crossing to a stile in the opposite field boundary in each case. In the fourth field, cross to a stile in the far right corner, before heading across the fifth field to a stile in the middle of the opposite field boundary. Cross field 6 to a stile in the

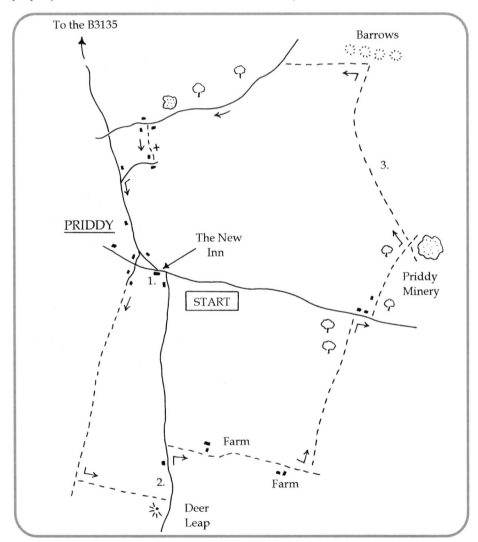

end field boundary, before following the left edge of the next field to a stone slab stile on the left in the corner. Cross this stile to enter an area of open access land. Walk across what is a hillside to a gate in the far left corner to reach the Deer Leap parking area and a lane.

2 Turn left along the lane and, in 600 yards, right along the track leading to Ebbor Grove Farm. Walk along to the farm and, in another 150 yards, keep on the track as it bears left. Continue along the track for another ¾ mile to a handgate on the left and a Monarch's Way waymark – this handgate is some 150 yards beyond Higher Pitts Farm, which is passed on the right. Pass through the handgate, and follow the left edges of four fields before joining the Priddy to Wells road. Turn right for 150 yards and, immediately past Rose Cottage, turn left along the driveway leading to Underbarrow Farm. Follow the path up past a caving club bungalow called the Belfry to a stile, cross a driveway to a stile opposite and follow the footpath – it immediately bears left – through the conifers along the edge of Priddy Minery. Continue along this path to a junction by a beech tree, before turning left to follow the course of an old wall uphill onto North Hill. Continue uphill to a stile in the top corner of the minery enclosure and enter an open hilltop field.

3 Follow the left edge of the hilltop field ahead to a handgate in the corner, before crossing the next field to reach a line of round barrows. Turn left and follow the line of barrows and, having passed the last tumulus, continue downhill to a gate in the bottom field boundary some 200 yards to the left of some coniferous

Priddy Green, scene of the annual sheep fair

trees. Join a tarmac lane, and follow it to the left for ½ mile towards Priddy. On reaching the edge of the village, turn left along a driveway between properties to reach a gate, and cross the field ahead to a gateway opposite and Priddy churchyard. Follow the path away from the church down past the local school to a lane, turn right to a minor junction by a green and then left down to the main road. Turn left and follow this road into Priddy, crossing the green at journey's end to reach the New Inn.

Place of Interest
Cheddar, with its caves and inland cliffs, lies just 5 miles west of Priddy. There are many other attractions in the village including a Cheddar Cheese Factory, a crazy golf course and a museum dedicated to the area's exceptional geological features. There are also all manner of tourist shops and businesses, many of which sell scrumpy cider, Somerset's favourite beverage! Telephone the local Tourist Information Centre on 01934 744071 for more details.

Date walk completed:

....

Wookey Hole

The Wookey Hole Inn

Wookey Hole village, with its fine show caves, is one of the great attractions of the Mendips. Any feelings of claustrophobia, however, will soon disappear as you climb over 700 feet onto the bare and open hilltops that tower above the village. What makes this walk particularly exciting is the rocky scramble that the path takes down through Ebbor Gorge towards journey's end. This dry Mendip valley, whose caves once sheltered wolves, bears and ancient peoples, is not for the faint hearted! The woodland at the foot of the gorge – all part of a National Nature Reserve – contains ash and elm, beech and oak, together with herbaceous plants such as dog's mercury, enchanter's nightshade and hart's tongue fern. The views from the hilltops above the gorge reach deep into the Somerset Levels, although the eye will inevitably be drawn towards Glastonbury Tor, the very heart of Avalon.

The **Wookey Hole Inn** has earned an enviable reputation since its recent refurbishment and renovation. It is difficult to describe just how different this unique establishment is but, with a walled sculpture garden planted with herbs, grasses and bamboos that is backlit at night, you might begin to get a feel of the character of this hostelry. The publicity material talks of 'an explosion of taste, colour and texture awaiting visitors, as well as the widest Belgium beer range on draught in England, the best in real ale plus fantastic food using the most local and free-range products.' What more could one ask?

Opening times are 12 noon to 3 pm and 6 pm to 11 pm on Monday to Saturday; 12 noon to 4 pm on Sunday.

Telephone: 01749 676677; website: www.wookeyholeinn.com

Distance: *5 miles*

OS Explorer 141 Cheddar Gorge and Mendip Hills West
GR 532475

Hill walking on Mendip, including a steep ascent and a rocky scramble down through Ebbor Gorge

Starting point: The Wookey Hole Inn.

How to get there: Initially make for Wells, on the main A39 road running from Bath to Bridgwater. Wookey Hole, being a major tourist attraction, is clearly signposted from Wells. There is limited roadside parking outside the inn – a better alternative is to use the large free car park, lying opposite, for visitors to Wookey Hole.

The Walk

① Exit the car park, turn left and, in 30 yards, on a sharp left-hand bend, turn right to follow a steep footpath signposted to Wells. On reaching a kissing gate by some cottages, continue along a short section of enclosed path to a stone slab stile. Follow the right edge of the field ahead to a stile in the corner, before crossing the next field to reach a handgate and a lane in Lower Milton. Turn left and follow the lane for ½ mile to a drive on the right leading down to a farm complex called Model Farm, just past a point where the lane crosses a stream. Go over a stile on the left here and follow the left edge of a small field to a stile and some woodland. Continue along the path ahead, with the stream on the left, for 350 yards to a track at the far end of the woodland. Walk ahead for a few yards to a pair of gates, pass through the right-hand gateway and head diagonally uphill across the field ahead to a stile in the top corner and the Old Bristol Road.

② Turn left and follow this lane uphill for 400 yards to a stile on the left by a metal gate. Cross the stile, and follow the line of the fence on the left steeply uphill to the hilltop before crossing to a stile in the corner of a field and joining a track. Turn left along to a bungalow, then continue along the hilltop track to a right-hand bend and a cattle grid. Beyond this grid, turn left into a hilltop field and head diagonally across the middle of the field – fine views to the south – to a handgate in the wall on the far side of the field. Cross the next field – bearing slightly right – to a gate in the opposite field boundary, then head directly across the next field to a stile in

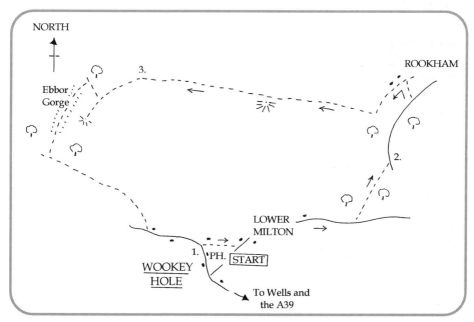

the opposite boundary. Follow the right edges of the next three fields to reach a gate and water trough in the corner of the third field. Do not go through the gate – instead turn left and follow the line of the fence on the right down to a gate and stile at the entrance to the Ebbor Gorge Reserve.

The impressive Ebbor gorge

❸ Follow the grassy path ahead down to a gate and stile, turn left and follow a prominent path down through the woodland to a junction in 200 yards where a path goes off on the right. (**NB:** Detour ahead at this point for 200 yards to reach a magnificent viewpoint high above Ebbor Gorge.) Turn right, walk downhill for a short distance into a valley bottom and turn left to follow the path that drops downhill through Ebbor Gorge itself. In 500 yards, at a junction, turn left and follow a woodland path for 250 yards to a gate at the exit from the reserve. Walk the whole length of the narrow field ahead, keeping right at the far end to reach a gate and a lane in Wookey Hole. Turn left and follow the road back into the village centre and the car park.

Date walk completed:

....

Places of Interest

Wookey Hole Caves, carved out of the limestone by the subterranean River Axe, provide an exciting underground tour, with seemingly innocuous limestone formations transformed into creatures of legend by highly imaginative tour guides! One pair of stalagmites is allegedly the petrified remains of a witch and her dog, turned into stone when doused in holy water by a monk. A visit to a traditional paper mill, a fine collection of fairground memorabilia, a small waxworks and a penny arcade are also on offer. Telephone 01749 672243 for further details.

The **City of Wells**, just 2 miles from Wookey Hole, is located deep within the heart of rural Somerset. With a population of just 10,000, Wells is England's smallest city. This peaceful and friendly settlement is steeped in heritage, boasting one of the finest cathedrals in Europe and countless ancient buildings, largely unchanged since their construction hundreds of years ago. For further information on the city's attractions, visit the Tourist Information Centre in the Market Place or telephone 01749 672552.

The King's Arms

Litton lies on the fringes of East Mendip, a landscape characterised by gentle hills and lush valleys. To the north of the village, hidden away by folds in the hills, lie two secluded reservoirs formed by damming the River Chew. This circuit explores the village of Litton and its neighbouring reservoirs, as well as the open expanses of Shortwood Common and Coley Hill, both locations bringing with them quite exceptional views. The reservoirs are a haven for wildfowl, with the various species to be spotted including little grebe and cormorant, tufted duck and goosander. With the fine outlook across the Somerset landscape, as well as the chance of a spot of bird watching, field glasses are a must on this particular walk.

The **King's Arms,** whose history can be traced back as far as the 15th century, is a fascinating old hostelry. Descend a flight of steps from the car park and you enter a world of polished flagstones and heavy beams, vast fireplaces and welcoming settles – a real sense of history pervades this ancient inn. There is even a suit of armour in an alcove in one of the bar areas. In addition to sandwiches and salads, the dishes available include lamb cutlets, king prawns and pork ribs, each served with tasty sauces. With a glass of Wadworth 6X or Bass to complement your meal, the King's Arms will provide welcome refreshment at journey's end.

Opening times are 11 am to 3 pm and 6 pm to 11 pm on Monday to Saturday; 12 noon to 4 pm on Sunday.

Telephone: 01761 241301.

Distance: *3½ miles*

OS Explorer 141 Cheddar Gorge and Mendip Hills West
GR 594545

A relatively easy walk, with one climb across Shortwood Common and a descent of Coley Hill

Starting point: The King's Arms car park in Litton - but do ask the landlord's permission first.

How to get there: Leave the A39 Bath to Wells road at Chewton Mendip, and follow the B3114 for 1 mile into Litton. The King's Arms is alongside the main road.

The Walk

1 Walk to the far end of the car park and drop down a bank to a lane. Turn right and follow the lane around to the village hall in Litton. Immediately before the hall, turn left along a track to a gate and stile. Follow the left edges of two fields ahead and, in a third field, walk around the edge of a water board installation to a stile in the fence on the left and a lane. Follow the lane to the right and, in 400 yards, keep on the lane as it bears left immediately past a cottage. In 150 yards, at a junction, turn left and follow the side lane uphill across Shortwood Common. Having reached Shortwood House at the top of the hill,

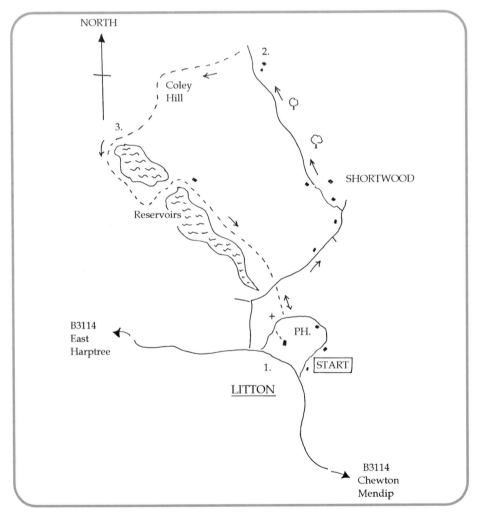

NORTH

Coley
Hill

2.

SHORTWOOD

Reservoirs

3.

B3114
East
Harptree

PH.

1.

START

LITTON

B3114
Chewton
Mendip

continue along the hilltop lane for ¾ mile to a stile and footpath on the left, immediately past Ham Farm.

2 Cross this stile, and head half-left across the field ahead to a stile in the left-hand field boundary. In the following field, bear half-right to a stile 100 yards along the right-hand field boundary from the corner of the field. Follow the line of the electricity wires across the next field to a stile just to the left of a telegraph pole. Walk diagonally downhill across the middle of the following field to a stile in the far right-hand corner, some 300 yards distant. Beyond this stile, turn right and follow the field boundary on the right down to a stile in the bottom field boundary and the banks of the lower reservoir at Litton.

3 Cross the dam ahead, an overflow channel and a cattle grid before going through the first gate on the left. Follow the left edge of the field ahead, with the banks of the lower reservoir beyond the hedge on the left, to a stile in the corner of the field. Follow the field boundary of the next field around to a footbridge over a stream in the far right corner. Beyond this stream, follow a woodland path alongside a stream down to Litton's lower reservoir

One of Litton's two reservoirs

before continuing along the path alongside the lake. Keep on this path as it eventually climbs to cross the dam at the foot of the upper reservoir. Cross this dam and, on the far side of the lake, follow the footpath to the right alongside the northern bank of the upper reservoir. In ½ mile, pass through a handgate to join a lane. Turn left, walk past the water board installation passed at the outset and cross a stile on the right. Retrace your steps across the right edges of three fields back to the village hall and lane in Litton, turn right and return to the King's Arms.

Date walk completed:

....

Places of Interest

Chew Valley Lake lies 5 miles north-west of Litton. This vast reservoir, some 2½ miles long and with a capacity of 4,500 million gallons, was opened by the Queen in 1956. As well as supplying water, Chew is a vast leisure amenity for fishermen, sailors and ornithologists. At the northern end of the reservoir – and signposted from surrounding roads – you will find a visitor centre and café. Telephone 01275 332339 for more information.

The Stanton Drew Stone Circles are just a few miles north of Litton. Here we find three circles: the Great circle being one of the largest such relics in the country. Were it not for the off-the-beaten track location of Stanton Drew, these stone circles would be of national renown.

The Talbot Inn

East Mendip, the countryside between Wells and Frome, lies well away from the main tourist honeypots of the Mendip Hills. While the landscape may lack the spectacular natural features found at Cheddar and Wookey, there is a much greater sense of human history in this corner of the hills. Mells, just a few miles west of Frome, is widely held to be among the most beautiful villages in Somerset. If the cottages with their 'holy greyness' were not enough, there is the magnificent church of St Andrew, lying alongside the Tudor manor house of the Horner family. While the manor is where the aristocrats ruled supreme, the valley of the Mells Stream was home to an altogether different family, the Fussells. These were industrialists, 19th century iron-masters, a complete contrast to the landed gentry up in the village. To escape from Mells and its ruling dynasties, this walk takes us onto Barrow Hill, a fine viewpoint over this far-flung corner of north-eastern Somerset.

The **Talbot Inn**, a 15th century coaching inn decorated with hanging baskets and tubs, is reached through large double doors under an archway that leads into an informally planted, cobbled courtyard. Renowned for the quality of its food, the Talbot offers ploughman's and ciabatta sandwiches, as well as more substantial dishes that include chicken liver parfait with spiced apple chutney or pork and chicken terrine with apricot and orange.

Opening times are 12 noon to 2.30 pm and 6.30 pm to 11 pm on weekdays; 12 noon to 3 pm and 6.30 pm to 11 pm on Saturday; 12 noon to 3 pm and 7 pm to 10.30 pm on Sunday.

Telephone: 01373 812254; website: www.talbotinn.com

Distance: *5 miles*

OS Explorer 142 Shepton Mallet and Mendip Hills East
GR 727492

Fieldpaths, lanes and tracks that cross an undulating landscape

Starting point: The Talbot Inn at Mells.

How to get there: Two miles from Frome on the A362 Radstock road, follow the unclassified road signposted to Great Elm and Mells. In 2½ miles, at a road junction in Mells, turn right and drive up past the village store and on for 350 yards to reach the Talbot Inn.

The Walk

1 Follow the side street alongside the Talbot Inn to Mells church, walk around to the back of the church and follow a path running between yew trees to a gate and open field. Cross this field to a stile in the middle of the opposite field boundary and, in the next field, cross to a gap in the hedgerow opposite before walking to the left around the following field to reach a stile and lane in the far left corner. Follow this lane around to the left, and on up Conduit Hill to reach a bridge over the former Radstock to Frome railway. About 150 yards beyond this railway bridge, follow a footpath – there is a marker post – into a field on the right. Follow the left edge of this field around to a stile in the far left corner, then cross a track and stile opposite before bearing half-right in the next field across to the right-hand field

boundary. Follow this field boundary for 300 yards to a stile at the far end of the field. Cross this stile, bear left in the next field and walk across to a gateway in the top corner of the field and a track.

2 Follow this track ahead for 100 yards, before following some steps on the right up to a handgate. Follow the footpath ahead, keeping a fence on the left and, where this fence ends, keep walking ahead, passing Hill House Farm on the left. Enter the field beyond the farm buildings and, part way across this field, pass through a gateway and join an enclosed track. Follow this track for 400 yards to reach a wooden fence and arable field, crossing one stile along the way. Follow the left edge of this hilltop field across Barrow Hill to its corner, before bearing right for 30 yards to reach a stile in the end field boundary. Drop downhill

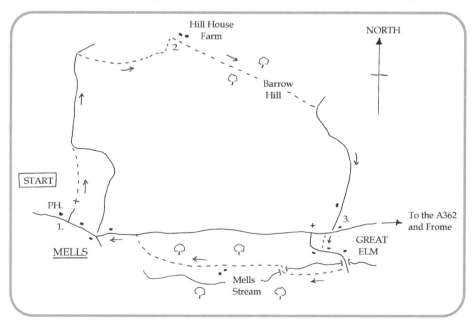

25

to a stile in the bottom right corner of the next field, pass through the corner of a small woodland and walk down the right edge of the next field to a gate and track. Follow this track for 175 yards to a lane, turn right and follow this lane for 600 yards to a junction with the main road in Great Elm.

3 Turn right and, in 150 yards, cross to a bollard on the left and follow a track downhill

Mells and its village shop

to a back lane in Great Elm. Follow the lane to the left around to the Mells Stream and, having crossed the river, pass through a handgate on the right and follow a track through the trees to some gates and a mineral railway line. Cross a footbridge on the right, keep right at an immediate fork and follow a path down to the Mells Stream again. Follow the riverside path upstream – ignoring all left turns – for 350 yards to a footbridge. Cross the river, turn left and continue following the Mells Stream upstream. On emerging from the woodland, cross a patch of grass to reach a drive, follow this drive ahead and, where this drive

forks right uphill, follow a lower enclosed path alongside the river. Continue on this path for 600 yards to the Great Elm to Mells road, detouring to the left at the end of a wall if you wish to explore Fussell's Ironworks, where the remains of the waterwheels and sluices, workshops and offices are still to be seen. Turn left, follow the road to a junction in Mells, turn right past the village shop and walk back through the village to the Talbot Inn.

Date walk completed:

....

Place of Interest

Frome Museum houses a fascinating collection of local artefacts and sources of information, ranging from costumes from the Horner family to glass negatives from Singers Art Metal works. It has a library, a collection of historic maps and a range of local information leaflets and books. Telephone 01373 463494 for more details or visit www.fromemuseum.org.uk

The Fox & Badger

square, the scene overlooked by the magnificent St Julian's church in the Somerset Perpendicular style. Below the village lies a picturesque ford alongside an ancient packhorse bridge, with a measuring pole suggesting that on occasions the water level can rise to as much as six feet above the road surface! Of even greater antiquity than the packhorse bridge is Stony Littleton Long Barrow, a Neolithic tomb used for collective burial that dates back to 2000 BC. With the magnificent natural landscape that stands as a backdrop to the whole scene, this is an absolutely delightful walk.

The North Somerset countryside really does offer the walker something a bit special. On this walk, for example, there is the village of Wellow, clinging to a south-facing hillside above the Wellow Brook. Its handsome properties are grouped around the village

Distance: *6 miles*

OS Explorer 142 Shepton Mallet and Mendip Hills East
GR 740583

Tracks, fieldpaths and lanes that cross a moderately hilly landscape

Starting point: The village square in Wellow by the Fox & Badger pub.

How to get there: Follow the B3110 road to the south of Bath. At Hinton Charterhouse, head west along the unclassified road signposted to Wellow. Follow this lane for 3 miles to the middle of Wellow, where the Fox and Badger lies alongside the village square.

The **Fox & Badger** exudes a traditional and unspoilt atmosphere. There is a public bar and a lounge, with flagstone flooring, open fireplaces and wooden beams lending a rustic feel. Should you visit the inn on a warm day, a pair of bench seats attached to the outside walls will enable you to take refreshment whilst enjoying the view of Wellow's main street. The menu is extensive, with the exceptional ploughman's lunches coming highly recommended. A fine range of real ales, including Draught Bass and Butcombe Bitter, is always available.

Opening times are 11.30 am to 3.30 pm and 6 pm to 11 pm on Monday to Thursday; 11.30 am to 11 pm on Friday and Saturday; 12 noon to 10.30 pm on Sunday.

Telephone: 01225 832293; website: www.foxandbadger.co.uk

The Walk

❶ With your back to the Fox & Badger, turn right and walk along Wellow's main street for 80 yards, then turn right down Mill Lane. Just before the ford at the foot of the hill, cross a stile on the left and walk the length of a meadow to a stile in the middle of the end field boundary. Cross to stiles in the far right corners of the next two fields before crossing a footbridge on the right halfway across the following field. Beyond this bridge, bear half-left across a hillside field to a handgate in the left-hand field boundary before bearing half-right in the next field to a stile in the right-hand field boundary. Beyond this stile, follow the right edge of the field ahead to a gate and lane by Wellow Farm. Turn left and follow the lane for 350 yards to a point where there are gates either side of the road. Pass through the gate on the right, the gatepost carrying a bridleway sign.

❷ Follow the track ahead to a pylon and continue to a corner formed by a fence. Follow the line of the fence to the left, walking parallel to the pylons on the left. In 120 yards, pass through a gate on the right and follow a path across the hillside, with an old fence on the left. Continue to the corner of the field before turning right up the end field boundary. Lower Baggridge Farm is ahead on the hilltop. Pass through a handgate on the left, cross the next field to a handgate ahead and follow the left edge of the following field to a gate and track. Turn right and follow this track for ½ mile to Upper Baggridge Farm,

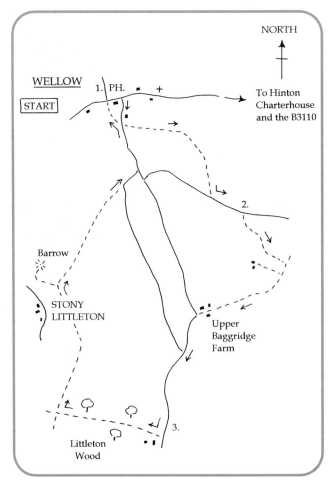

WELLOW
START
1. PH.
NORTH
To Hinton Charterhouse and the B3110
2.
Barrow
STONY LITTLETON
Upper Baggridge Farm
3.
Littleton Wood

ignoring an early right turn to Lower Baggridge Farm. Go through a gate before the farm, walk through the farmyard and go through a second gate to join the lane beyond the farmhouse. Follow this lane ahead for 1 mile across the hilltop and, just before an isolated property, turn right along a byway into Littleton Wood.

Stoney Littleton Long Barrow

3 Follow this byway downhill for ½ mile to a crossroads and a marker post. Turn right and follow a bridleway across three fields to reach a ruinous barn on the hillside. Continue past this barn to a handgate on the left, at the point where the hedgerow ends. Beyond this handgate, follow the field boundary on the right downhill to the bottom corner of the field by Wellow Brook. Cross a stile on the right, and follow the line of the hedge on the left uphill to a gate in the top corner. (**NB:** To visit Stony Littleton Long Barrow, cross a stile on the left just before the top corner of the field, follow the hedge on the right for 200 yards to another stile and head uphill to the barrow.) Follow the line of the hedge beyond this gate across the hilltop and, where the hedge ends, continue across the hilltop to a gateway opposite. Continue along an enclosed track for 400 yards to a lane. Follow the lane ahead to a junction in just a few yards, and turn left down to the ford in Wellow. Cross the packhorse bridge to the left of the ford, and walk along the gravel track ahead, uphill to a

gateway and the trackbed of the old Somerset and Dorset railway. Cross to the gateway opposite, and follow a lane back to the Square in Wellow.

Place of Interest

To the south-west of Wellow, the **Radstock Museum**, housed in the former Market Hall in the centre of Radstock, contains a unique collection of local artefacts, photographs, documents and books relating to the North Somerset Coalfield. These include a reconstructed coalface, a miner's kitchen, a 1930s Co-op shop and a Victorian schoolroom. The museum is open from 2 pm until 5 pm each day – apart from Mondays – but is closed throughout December and January. Telephone 01761 437722 for further details of this quite excellent community museum.

Date walk completed:

. . . .

Freshford

The Inn at Freshford

Freshford lies on the extreme southern boundary of the Cotswolds, a few miles outside Bath, in an area that has only recently been included in the AONB. The village is clearly Cotswold in character, however, with its golden cottages and houses, its historic associations with the woollen trade and its location amidst rolling hills and river valleys. The walk features everything that is best about this region of Britain, the rivers, valleys and green rolling hills forming an excellent backdrop for attractive stone villages, historic churches and country houses, including the manors at both Westwood and Iford. There is also an element of industrial archaeology along the way at Avoncliff, where a noted aqueduct carries the Kennet and Avon Canal across the River Avon in a most spectacular setting. This is truly a walk with a surprise at every turn!

The **Inn at Freshford** overlooks the Somerset Frome, a sparkling tributary of the Bristol Avon. It is a picturesque three-storey stone building, attractively decorated with window boxes, hanging baskets and tubs of flowers. Dating from Tudor times, the inn has been comfortably modernised without losing its traditional character. Exposed beams and stonework are testament to the age of this fine old hostelry. The excellent food ranges from sandwiches and ploughman's through to more substantial offerings such as steak and ale pie and fish specials, whilst the real ales might typically include Wadworth 6X and Butcombe Bitter. On a fine summer's day, the inn's pretty garden is one of the more popular resting-places in the area.

Opening times are 11 am to 3 pm and 6 pm to 11 pm every day.

Telephone: 01225 722250.

Distance: 6 miles

OS Explorers 142 Shepton Mallet and Mendip Hills East and 156 Chippenham and Bradford-on-Avon
GR 791600

Fieldpaths, tracks and quiet lanes crossing a landscape of hills and valleys

Starting point: The Inn at Freshford.

How to get there: Leave the A36 at Monkton Combe, 5 miles south of Bath, and follow the B3108 towards Bradford-on-Avon. In ½ mile, just before a railway bridge, turn right into Limpley Stoke village. Follow the road for 1½ miles through to Freshford, where the Inn at Freshford lies on the southern edge of the village, just before the River Frome. Park on the roadside in the vicinity of the inn, or ask the landlord's permission to use the car park.

The Walk

1 With your back to the inn, turn right and in a few yards turn right again through a gate to follow a signposted footpath. In 50 yards, keep on the path as it bears right uphill into woodland. Pass through a gate at the top of the climb, turn left and continue following the woodland path above the Frome downhill to a gate by the river. Cross the field ahead to the next gate before going over a meadow to a gate and quiet lane. Turn right and, in 150 yards, follow a bridleway on the left around to the frontage of Middle House. Turn left at this point, and follow an enclosed track across the valley side for 500 yards to a handgate on the edge of Friary. Drop downhill across an open area of grassland to join the lane in this diminutive rural hamlet.

2 Turn left and, in 20 yards, right along a path across open grassland opposite a property called Whistlers Hollow to a gateway and field. Cross this field to reach a gate at the entrance to Friary Wood, and follow the main woodland path through to a gate and riverside meadow. Walk the whole length of this meadow to a stile in the far right corner, join a lane and turn left into Iford, crossing the Frome to reach a junction in front of Iford Manor. Turn right uphill and, in 120 yards, fork right along a bridleway. Follow this enclosed track for ½ mile through to the Farleigh Hungerford to Westwood lane. Turn left and, in 500 yards, cross a stile on the right to join a waymarked footpath. Follow the path through a recently planted copse, before following the left edges of two fields around to a stile opposite Westwood Manor and church.

3 Cross the stile opposite Westwood Manor and church and follow the lane to the right to a junction in the village by the

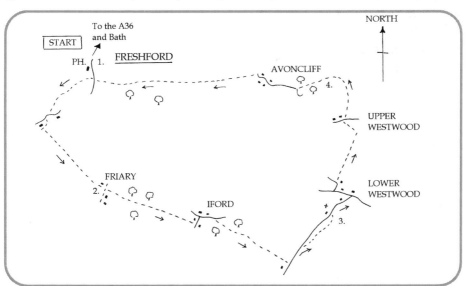

New Inn. Turn left and, in 300 yards, take the right turn to Upper Westwood and Avoncliff. In 50 yards, on a left-hand bend, cross the stile ahead and follow a footpath across the right edges of three fields to a stone stile in the right corner of the third field. Beyond this stile, turn left and walk across to a clearly visible stile in the right corner of the end field boundary. Cross and join a lane, before passing through the gateway opposite – slightly to the right – to enter a field. Walk down the left edge of this field – with a bungalow on the left – to a stile in the bottom field boundary, before following the left edge of the following field to another stile. Drop downhill in the next field, passing to the left of a telegraph pole, to a stile and a field immediately above the Kennet and Avon Canal. Follow the path that bears left across the top of this field around to a gate at the entrance to woodland.

The River Avon

❹ Follow the main path through the woodland for 600 yards to a lane, and follow the lane to the right downhill into the canalside hamlet of Avoncliff. Immediately past the Mad Hatter Tea Rooms, turn left along an unmetalled track that passes a former Poor House that has now been converted into apartments. Just past this building, pass through a gate ahead and follow an enclosed path above the River Avon along to the next handgate. Walk the length of the riverside meadow ahead to a stile on the far side of the field, and continue along an enclosed path running between the river and woodland to a kissing gate and large open field. Walk diagonally across the middle of this field to a gate in its far right corner, join a lane and turn right to return to the Inn at Freshford.

Date walk completed:

. . . .

Places of Interest

Westwood Manor, a 15th century stone manor house, was altered in the early 17th century and has late Gothic and Jacobean windows and fine plasterwork. There is also a modern topiary garden. This National Trust property opens on Tuesdays, Wednesdays and Sundays between 2 pm and 5 pm from April through to September. Telephone 01225 863374 for details.

The **Peto Garden at Iford Manor** is a grade I Italian-style garden famous for its tranquil beauty. The manor was the home of the architect and landscape gardener Harold A. Peto from 1899 to 1933. This unique and romantic hillside garden is characterised by steps, terraces, sculpture and magnificent rural views. It is open during April and October on Sundays and Easter Monday between 2 pm and 5 pm and from May to September daily between 2 pm and 5 pm except on Mondays and Fridays. Telephone: 01225 863146.

The climbs encountered in the course of this walk on the Somerset/Wiltshire border are more than compensated for by a series of fine vantage points – south from Monkton Farleigh towards Salisbury Plain, north from Kingdown across the

Distance: 5 miles

OS Explorers 155 Bristol and Bath and 156 Chippenham and Bradford-on-Avon GR 804653

An undulating landscape, with a climb of nearly 600 feet from Bathford church to Brown's Folly

Starting point: The King's Arms in Monkton Farleigh.

How to get there: Leave the A4 at Bathford, 3 miles east of Bath, and follow the A363 towards Bradford-on-Avon. In 3 miles, turn left along the road signposted to Monkton Farleigh. In 1 mile, at a junction in the village, turn left and the King's Arms is on the left. Park on the roadside nearby.

By Brook Valley towards Colerne and west from Bathford across the Avon Valley towards Bath. As well as the fine views, there is ample opportunity to explore the Brown's Folly Nature Reserve, an area of cool deciduous woodland and open limestone grassland. A Mr Wade-Brown allegedly constructed the folly, high on the hilltop, when recession was hitting the fortunes of his local quarrying company. Easily visible from Bath, the vast stone tower was an advertisement for the quality of his fine stone, much of which formed the building blocks of Georgian Bath.

The **King's Arms** in Monkton Farleigh dates from the 11th century, with exposed stonework and ancient beams bearing testimony to its age. Beyond the beautiful courtyard and magnificent entrance porch lie the Chancel Restaurant and the public bar, where visitors will find a welcoming log fire during winter months. To the rear of the inn there is a delightful garden, where dishes from the bar or garden menu can be enjoyed along with a glass of local real ale such as Wadworth 6X or Butcombe Bitter. Several ghostly tales are connected with this old hostelry. One tells how a woman can be heard wailing pitifully on the anniversary of her death, a fatality caused by her runaway coach crashing into the wall of the inn.

Opening times are 12 noon to 3 pm and 5.30 pm to 11 pm on Monday to Friday; 12 noon to 11 pm on Saturday; 12 noon to 10.30 pm on Sunday.

Telephone: 01225 858705.

The Walk

1 Take the turning just below the King's Arms signposted to Kingsdown and Bath. In 250 yards, keep on the lane as it bears right by Home Farm and, in 100 yards, pass through a gateway on the left to follow a signposted footpath. Follow the right edge of the field ahead – with views on the right towards Salisbury Plain – to a stile before continuing along an enclosed path to a lane. Cross a stile opposite, and follow the right edge of the next field, then continue along an enclosed path that borders woodland to reach a stile. Cross the field ahead, passing to the left of a pond, and come to the corner of Ashley Wood. Walk down the edge of the woodland – with the trees on the left – for 150 yards before bearing right to

reach the end of a wall. Beyond this point, turn right to reach a gate and stile 40 yards ahead. On the other side of this gate, follow a grassy track along the left edge of a field and down past some properties to reach the Kingsdown to Bathford road.

2 Turn left for 100 yards, then right just before the Swan Inn into Lower Kingsdown Road. Drop downhill for 50 yards, turn left at a junction and continue for 200 yards before turning right into Wormcliffe Lane. Drop downhill for 200 yards, then turn left along a signposted bridleway. Follow this enclosed track for ¾ mile through to Bathford – where the track becomes a metalled lane – and continue ahead to a junction with Bathford Hill. Turn right and, in 100

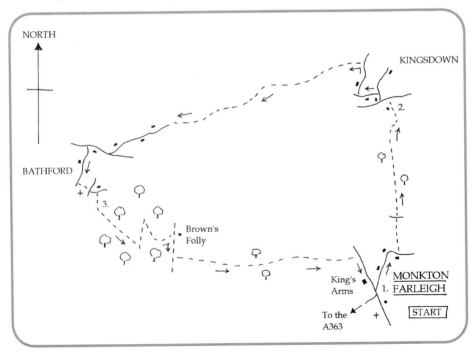

yards, left into Church Street. Continue for 350 yards and, immediately before the entrance to St Swithun's church, turn left and follow an enclosed path uphill alongside the churchyard to reach a back lane in Bathford. Turn right and almost immediately left into Mountain Wood. Where this road bears left into an estate, keep ahead across a grassy area to reach a stile in the hedge on the right. Cross this stile, and head diagonally across the field ahead uphill to a stile at the entrance to the Brown's Folly Reserve.

Brown's Folly sits high on the hilltop

❸ Head uphill through the woodland, keeping to the right-hand lower path where the right of way divides to form two parallel routes. Continue to a junction, turn left to follow a level path across the bottom edge of a hillside

Place of Interest

Monkton Farleigh lies just 4 miles from **Bradford-on-Avon**, one of the finest small towns in England. Visitors to this delightful settlement will find a Saxon church and an ancient tithe barn, a lock-up on the magnificent Town Bridge and serried ranks of weavers' cottages clinging to the hillside above the river. There is also a charming museum, located above the Town Library, which offers displays that interpret the local townscape and its history. The town's Tourist Information Centre can be contacted on 01225 865797.

clearing and, at the next junction, turn right up to a gateway and continue across the open hillside ahead. On the far side of this open area, just before a gate, turn left and follow a stepped path uphill to a track on the hilltop, just below Brown's Folly. Turn right and, on reaching an information board in 200 yards, turn left along an enclosed path to a gate and open field. Follow the uncultivated strip of grass across this field to a track, turn left and, in the middle of a small copse, follow a path on the right through the trees to reach a back lane. Cross the stile opposite, and follow the right edge of the field ahead towards a chimney stack. Beyond the gate on the far side of the field continue along a grassy track down to a gate and lane. Turn right back into Monkton Farleigh, reaching the King's Arms in 300 yards.

Date walk completed:

....

Whether it be driving down Widcombe Hill into the centre of Bath, strolling along Bristol's Park Street or walking the hilltops above the Westbury White Horse in Wiltshire, Kelston Round Hill always seems to crop up somewhere in the distance. This ubiquitous landmark, with a small spinney atop its lofty summit, is arguably the best-known physical feature in the Bath and Bristol region. The views from this lofty perch are as one would expect. Not only does the outlook encompass much of Bath and Bristol, there are also the Mendip Hills to the south, the Brecon Beacons to the west and the Wiltshire Downs away to the east. Below the Round Hill we find Kelston itself, where the church was the subject of inevitable Victorian 'improvement'. The village also boasts Tower House, a very private residence with a somewhat bizarre claim to fame. It was here that the water closet was allegedly invented. Sir John Harington, godson to Queen Elizabeth I, set about making a 'necessary' for his godmother and himself in 1596. A rather accomplished inventor, Harington ended his career with this discovery, for he was ridiculed by his peers for this absurd device. He never built another one, though he and his godmother both used theirs.

The **Old Crown Inn** is a cosy low-ceilinged hostelry that was originally an 18th century coaching inn. With its flagstone floor and church pew seats, as well as a beer engine in the main bar, this is an inn with a truly traditional feel and atmosphere. Being a Butcombe hostelry, Butcombe Bitter and Gold are two of the fine real ales that are available, in addition to other local ales such as Bath Gem and Wadworth 6X. The home-cooked meals are well known locally, and the Old Crown is a busy and popular inn. Children under 14 are not allowed inside.

Opening times are 11.30 am to 2.30 pm and 5 pm to 11 pm on Monday to Friday; 11.30 am to 11 pm on Saturday; 12 noon to 10.30 pm on Sunday.

Telephone: 01225 423032.

Distance: *4 miles*

OS Explorer 155 Bristol and Bath GR 700671

A climb onto the 700 foot summit of Kelston Round Hill is followed by a slow, gradual descent back into the village

Starting point: The lane leading to Kelston church.

How to get there: Kelston lies on the A431 Bristol road, 3 miles west of Bath. On a sharp bend in the village, by the clearly visible Tower House, turn into the cul-de-sac lane leading down to the church and park on the roadside.

The Walk

1 Return to the main road, turn left – passing the Old Crown Inn – and in 250 yards turn right along a cul-de-sac lane by Mill Barn Farm. Follow this lane uphill for 600 yards to Coombe Barn, bear right in front of this property and continue uphill along the byway for another 600 yards to a left-hand bend. At this point, bear right across the verge to a stile and follow the permissive footpath uphill to Kelston Round Hill. Follow the fence to the right around the clump of trees on the hilltop to a stile, and continue ahead to the trig point. Drop downhill to a stile in the bottom field boundary, and join the Cotswold Way. Follow this enclosed path to the right for ¾ mile.

2 Just before reaching a property, turn right along a gravelled track for 100 yards, cross a stile and follow the left edge of a field to the next stile in the corner of the field by Dean Hill House. In the following field, head across to a stile in the far left corner, where the field narrows. Head across to a gate in the

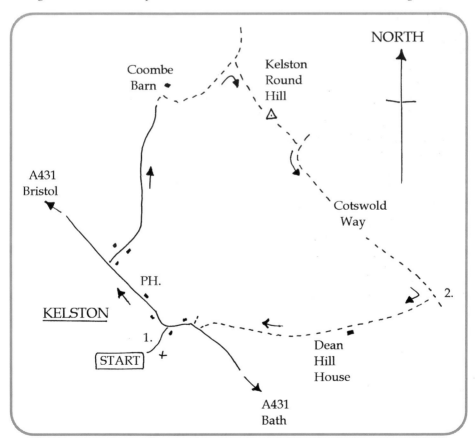

NORTH

Coombe Barn

Kelston Round Hill

A431 Bristol

Cotswold Way

PH.

KELSTON

2.

1.

START

Dean Hill House

A431 Bath

On the Cotswold Way

next field, just to the left of a barn. Follow the grassy path beyond this gate to a fork, then bear left downhill to the next gate. Keep straight ahead, walking between a brick building and a spring, to a gate and stile opposite, before continuing along a fieldpath to a gate on the far side of the field. Continue along a track down to the A431, before turning right back into Kelston.

Date walk completed:

....

Places of Interest

Bath is a World Heritage Site best known for its Roman Baths and fine Abbey, as well as a plethora of magnificent Georgian architecture. For further information, telephone the Tourist Information Line on 0906 711 2000.

The **Avon Valley Railway**, a 5 mile return train ride along the former Mangotsfield to Bath Green Park branch of the old Midland railway, is based at Bitton Station just a few miles west of Kelston. The former Midland Railway station has been painstakingly restored from a derelict site to provide visitors with refreshment and toilet facilities, a railway shop, a pleasant garden and outdoor seating. A wide variety of main line and industrial steam and diesel locomotives can be viewed in the former goods yard, along with carriages and wagons. Telephone 0117 932 5538 for more details; website: www.avonvalleyrailway.co.uk

The Catherine Wheel

The Cotswold Hills is something of a misnomer. In reality, there is an undulating plateau with a steep west-facing escarpment that drops down to the Severn Vale. Marshfield, a former coaching stop on the route from London to Bristol, is situated high on the Cotswold plateau. Attractive stone cottages and houses line the lengthy main street, which runs for over half a mile from a rank of almshouses dating from 1619 through to the parish church. Arthur Mee described West Littleton, hidden in a fold in the landscape north of Marshfield, as 'a small place very high'. Charming Cotswold properties are scattered around the delightful church, where a 700 year old bellcote stands proudly above the east gable of the nave. Between these two villages lies a swathe of former sheep pasture, open and exposed, with drystone walls and family-owned farms providing a most traditional feel to this delightful corner of South Gloucestershire.

The Catherine Wheel, a handsome Georgian hostelry, boasts a fine dining room. Walkers, however, may find the main bar – with its stripped stone walls and medley of settles, its open fireplace and prints – more to their liking. There is also a cosy patio garden. The inn started its life as a family home and became a pub at some point in the 1600s. It was originally called the Star and at that stage had its own malthouse and brewhouse. Today's customers are offered a wide choice of imaginative dishes, which might include pan-fried chicken breast served on a tarragon mash or whole mackerel baked with tapenade. Fine real ales are also available at the Catherine Wheel, including Abbey Bellringer brewed nearby in Bath.

Distance: 6 miles

OS Explorer 155 Bristol and Bath
GR 779737

Quiet lanes and fieldpaths that cross the undulating Cotswold plateau

Starting point: The Catherine Wheel at the eastern end of Marshfield's High Street.

How to get there: The A420 running between Bristol and Chippenham bypasses Marshfield. From this main road, the village centre is signposted. Drive to the eastern end of the High Street and park on the roadside in the vicinity of the Catherine Wheel.

Opening times on Monday to Saturday are 11 am to 3 pm (not Monday) and 6 pm to 11 pm; 12 noon to 3 pm and 7 pm to 10.30 pm on Sunday.

Telephone: 01225 892220.

The Walk

1 Walk westwards along Marshfield's High Street for 100 yards before turning right – immediately before Cotswold House – into Touching End Lane. At the top of this road, follow West Littleton Road around to the left to the A420. Cross this busy road with care, and follow the lane opposite for ½ mile to a crossroads. Turn left and, in 300 yards, at the next crossroads, turn right along the road signposted to Dyrham and Doynton. Follow this lane for ½ mile and, immediately before Springs Farm, cross a stile on the right to join a waymarked path.

2 Follow the path alongside a wall on the left to a stone slab stile at the top of the field, then walk ahead across the next field – with a wall on the right – before crossing a step stile over the wall at the end of the field. Drop downhill in the next field to a gate in the valley bottom, before

heading uphill – bearing slightly right all the while – to a gate in the top field boundary. Beyond this gate, follow a grassy track to the next gate and a lane. Turn left into West Littleton and, on reaching a telephone box, follow a gravel track on the left up to the church. Cross a stile on the far side of the churchyard, and follow an enclosed path alongside a horse exercise paddock to a gate and field. Cross this field to a gateway opposite, beyond which head across to a handgate on the left some 10 yards distant.

3 Beyond this handgate, follow the top left edge of a hillside field to a gap in the end field boundary, before following the top left edge of the next field to a wooden barrier on the left in the far corner. Cross this barrier, turn right and pass through a gateway to follow the left edges of two fields to reach a barn. Pass to the right of the barn and follow the edge of the field ahead to a gate in the corner. Walk ahead for a few yards alongside a copse to the

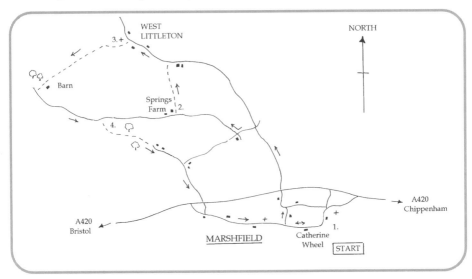

The 17th century almshouses in Marshfield

next gate and a lane. Turn left and follow this lane for ¾ mile. Where this lane bears left, fork right onto a bridleway.

4 Follow a track down to a gateway, before following the less distinct bridleway ahead through some tree cover. At the far side of the trees, enter an open field and drop downhill to a footbridge over a stream at the bottom of a slope. Pass through the gateway ahead, and follow a track uphill to reach a lane

by Westend Town Farm. Follow the lane ahead for 300 yards to a junction by a farmhouse. Follow the lane ahead past the farmhouse up to the A420. Continue along the lane opposite, down to the western end of Marshfield's main street. Turn left and follow the High Street back to the Catherine Wheel.

Date walk completed:

....

Place of Interest

Dyrham Park lies just a few miles north-west of Marshfield, alongside the A46 road heading to the M4 motorway. A mansion built for William Blathwayt, Secretary at War and Secretary of State to William III, the rooms have changed little since those days. Around the grand mansion stand 274 acres of parkland, which contain a herd of fallow deer. A National Trust property, the estate is open to the public between April and October. Telephone 01179 372501 for further details.

The White Hart

Cotswold architecture, the parish church and the market cross, the village has become justifiably popular with visitors to the area. This walk explores not only the village, but also some of the fine natural landscape surrounding it. This includes a dry river valley, splendid deciduous woodland, traditional meadows and the banks of the By Brook, a noted trout stream. Much of this landscape is a nature reserve managed by the Wiltshire Trust for Nature Conservation, and is therefore of quite exceptional quality. A fine ramble that proves that the Southwolds have much to offer for the rambler who believes that the 'wolds end at Cirencester!

Castle Combe is undoubtedly one of Britain's most attractive villages. Its golden cottages nestle at the foot of a charming valley, made even more beautiful by the sparkling waters of the By Brook. With all of the classic

Distance: *4 miles*

OS Explorer 156 Chippenham and Bradford-on-Avon
GR 842772

A relatively gentle walk, with just one or two short climbs. Be prepared for some mud after heavy rainfall

Starting point: The White Hart in Castle Combe.

How to get there: Leave the A420 between Bristol and Chippenham at Ford, on the A420, and follow the unclassified road to Castle Combe. The White Hart lies at the top of the main street by the village cross. There is room for limited parking outside the inn. Failing this, there is roadside parking 150 yards above it on the road to Upper Castle Combe.

The **White Hart** at Castle Combe is a charming old inn that overlooks the village cross in what is a picture postcard settlement. Inside the bar and family room, flagstone flooring, low ceilings, beams and open fireplaces lend this Cotswold hostelry a most traditional and welcoming feel. In addition to soup, sandwiches and jacket potatoes, customers can enjoy grilled steaks, baked and fried fish, home-made pies, curries and vegetarian dishes as well as daily specials. With a welcoming pint of Wadworth 6X or Farmers Glory to accompany your meal, the White Hart is certainly a pub in which to rest and linger awhile.

Opening times are 11 am to 3 pm and 6 pm to 11 pm. Food is normally served from 12 noon to 2 pm and from 7 pm to 9 pm.

Telephone: 01249 782295.

The Walk

1 Follow the road uphill out of Castle Combe from the White Hart for 250 yards before turning right opposite Hill House and the local museum to follow an enclosed sunken path. In 250 yards, at the top of a climb, turn left at a junction with

a back lane and continue for 200 yards to the B4039 in Upper Castle Combe. Follow the pavement opposite to the right for 100 yards, then turn left along a lane running alongside a local chapel. Follow this lane to a sharp left-hand bend in 600 yards and turn right along a byway called Summer Lane. Follow this byway

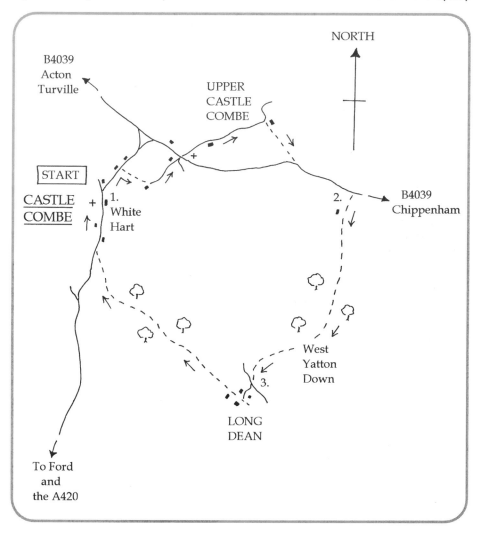

for 600 yards down to the B4039 before following the main road down past an entrance to Castle Combe Race Track and on for 100 yards to a handgate on the right and a signposted bridleway.

Castle Combe's famous market place

❷ Turn right through this gate, cross a field and join a drive running past a cottage. Beyond this cottage, continue along a track to a pair of gates. Pass through the left-hand gateway and drop downhill to a gate on the far side of the field. Continue through a shallow valley, following a gravelled track, to the next gateway before entering a nature reserve. Continue ahead to a clearing, walk across the right edge of this open space to the next gate and continue along a track through the valley bottom for 450 yards to the next gate. Pass to the right of the bushes ahead, and follow a path across the side of West Yatton Down, a delightful valley. At the far side of the valley, bear left and continue along the footpath to a handgate and lane.

❸ Turn left and, almost immediately, right along the cul-de-sac lane to Long Dean. At the junction in Long Dean by By Brook House, turn right and follow a track uphill out of Long Dean to a gateway almost on the hilltop. Continue ahead to a second gate, before following a track across a wooded hillside high above the By Brook. In ½ mile, having emerged into a more open hillside field, follow the path ahead along the bottom left edge of the field to a stile by the By Brook in its far

left corner. Continue alongside a short section of riverside path to a bridge, cross the river and join the road leading into Castle Combe. Follow this road to the right into the village and continue up the High Street to the White Hart.

Place of Interest
The nearest town to Castle Combe is **Chippenham**, originally a Saxon market place on the River Avon. The oldest part of the town lies around St Mary's church, where there are a number of half-timbered houses of the 16th and 17th centuries as well as stone-built Georgian properties. These historic dwellings reflect the town's former days as a cloth centre. The history of Chippenham can be discovered by visiting the Museum and Heritage Centre in the Market Place. Telephone 01249 705020 for details.

Date walk completed:
....

is known locally – provides some of the best-loved walking in the region. From Old Sodbury, where St John's church sits atop a small knoll overlooking the Severn Vale, fieldpaths and lanes are followed through to Horton, with its magnificent Court and adjoining church. From the sheltered villages down below, the walk returns to Old Sodbury across the escarpment. The views are fine – extending over the Severn Vale towards Wales – with the high wolds providing a final surprise in the form of Sodbury Fort.

The line of the Cotswold escarpment marks the divide between the high wolds, undulating former sheep pasture, and the Severn Vale, historically a landscape of prosperous dairy farms with the occasional apple orchard. Separated by several hundred feet of steep hillside, the Cotswold Edge – as it

Distance: 5 miles

OS Explorer 167 Thornbury, Dursley and Yate
GR 756818

Fieldpaths and quiet lanes in and around the steep Cotswold escarpment

Starting point: St John's church in Old Sodbury.

How to get there: Old Sodbury lies on the A432, which runs from the A46 through to Bristol via Chipping Sodbury and Yate. At the top of Cotswold Lane, the road opposite the Dog Inn, park outside St John's church.

The **Dog Inn** is situated directly alongside the busy A432 road, but step inside its two-level bar and you will find a cosy and welcoming hostelry with bare stone walls, beams and timbering, low ceilings, wall benches and open fireplaces. What is most remarkable about the Dog Inn, however, is its vast menu, which extends from sandwiches and ploughman's through to every conceivable type of main course. Add a good West Country ale – like Wickwar BOB – and you have the perfect resting-place following a stroll along the Cotswold escarpment.

Opening times are 11.30 am to 3 pm and 6 pm to 11 pm on Monday to Saturday; 12 noon to 4 pm and 7 pm to 10.30 pm on Sunday.

Telephone: 01454 312006.

The Walk

1 Walk through the churchyard, pass through a gate in the boundary wall and enter a hillside field by a topograph. Bear half-right, and head downhill to a stile in the right-hand field boundary, almost in the corner of the field. Follow the right edges of the next three fields, walking parallel to a power line, before following the right-hand field boundary of the next field around to a stile and lane. Cross this lane to a stile opposite, and enter a field that contains a number of pillow mounds. Cross to a stile in the far right corner of this field, and join the lane in Little Sodbury. Turn left, pass St Adeline's church and, at a junction, turn right. In 80 yards, turn left alongside a cottage to follow the waymarked Cotswold Way to a stile and open field.

2 Follow the bottom left-hand edges of the next two fields to a gate, then drop downhill in the next field – with a pond on the right – before continuing on uphill to a stile on the hilltop. Cross the middle of the next field, passing to the left of horse paddocks on the far side of the field, to a handgate and continue down a track to the lane in Horton. Turn right up to a junction by the local school, then turn left to follow the lane towards Horton Court. In ½ mile, a little way before Horton Court, cross a stile on the right to follow the Cotswold Way up the left edge of a field to a stile and woodland. (**NB:** Detour ahead along the lane to see the Court and church.)

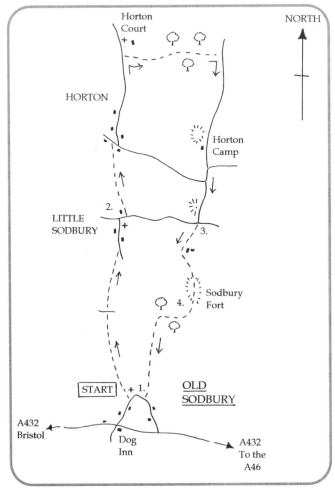

Walk uphill along the woodland path for 350 yards to a lane, then turn right and continue for ½ mile to a junction, passing the entrance to Horton Camp along the way. Follow the road ahead at this junction – signposted to Horton and Chipping Sodbury – and, in 50 yards, where the road bears right downhill, follow the side lane ahead for ½ mile to a junction.

The topograph near the start of the walk

❸ Cross the stepped stile opposite into a field, and head across to the next stile and a paddock in the far right corner. Follow the right edge of this paddock to a gravelled area by a converted farm building. Beyond the gate on the right, turn left along a grassy path by a converted barn. Where this barn ends, keep ahead through scrubland for 80 yards to a handgate on the left. Beyond this gate, keep ahead for 20 yards before turning right through the ramparts of Sodbury Fort. Cross the enclosure ahead to a gap in the opposite ramparts, then continue across the field to a handgate by some conifers.

❹ Beyond this gate, turn right and follow an enclosed sunken path downhill. At the foot of the slope, where this path bears right, pass through a gate on the left and follow the Cotswold Way across the top left edge of a field, with views to the west across the Severn Vale. Pass through a handgate in the far left corner of this field, before heading across the next field to a handgate in its corner on the edge of Old Sodbury. Continue along an enclosed path back to Cotswold Lane by Old Sodbury School, and turn right back to the church.

Date walk completed:

....

Place of Interest
At **Horton Court**, a Norman hall and an exceptionally fine detached ambulatory are all that remain of what is probably the oldest rectory in England. There are interesting early Renaissance features, including stucco caricatures of classical figures. This National Trust property is open to the public on Wednesdays and Saturdays between April and October from 2 pm to 6 pm. Telephone 01179 372501 for details.

Littleton upon Severn
The White Hart

This fine excursion explores part of the atmospheric Severn Estuary between Avonmouth and Gloucester. Although some distance from the river itself, Littleton would literally have been 'upon Severn' in centuries past, when floods frequently swamped the local low-lying land. From the village, fieldpaths and quiet lanes are followed through to neighbouring Oldbury on Severn where, from a seat in St Arilda's churchyard, a magnificent view across the Severn Vale opens up. It is the perfect spot to rest and linger awhile. The return to Littleton is quite literally along the banks of the great river, ending up at Whale Wharf. It was in this muddy inlet back in 1885 that a whale became stranded on the outgoing tide, an event that placed this remote spot into the national gaze.

The **White Hart** at Littleton, with its whitewashed walls and gabled windows, possesses a traditional and timeless feel. Wooden and tiled floors, rugs, wood panelling, exposed beams and a large open fireplace combine to lend a truly rustic atmosphere. The delicious food offerings range from baguettes through to barbecued chicken or mushroom and nut stroganoff whilst, being part of the Young's estate, fine real ales such as Young's Bitter and Special or Smiles Best are always available.

Opening times are 12 noon to 2.30 pm and 6 pm to 11 pm on Monday to Friday; 11 am to 2.30 pm and 6 pm to 11 pm on Saturday; 12 noon to 3 pm and 7 pm to 10.30 pm on Sunday.

Telephone: 01454 412275.

Distance: *5 miles*

OS Explorer 167 Thornbury, Dursley and Yate
GR 596901

A gentle and relaxing stroll, with the only ascent being onto the diminutive knoll that provides the location for St Arilda's church in Oldbury

Starting point: The White Hart in Littleton upon Severn.

How to get there: Leave the M48 at junction 1, near the first Severn Crossing, and follow the B4461, signposted to Thornbury. In 2 miles, in the village of Elberton, take the unclassified road signposted to Littleton upon Severn. In 1 mile, the White Hart lies on the right in the heart of the village, and there is room for careful roadside parking alongside the pub.

The Walk

1 With your back to the White Hart, follow the road to the right for 150 yards to a junction, and turn right along the road leading to Thornbury. In 300 yards, turn left along a track leading to St Mary's church. Follow this track along to the church, cross the stile directly ahead and walk beside the right edge of a field to a gate in its corner, all the while enjoying fine views of the Severn Vale. Continue at the right edge of the next field to a gate, before going along the right edge of the following field to a stile in its far right corner. Enter an orchard, and make for a point halfway down its right-hand boundary, then follow a footpath that

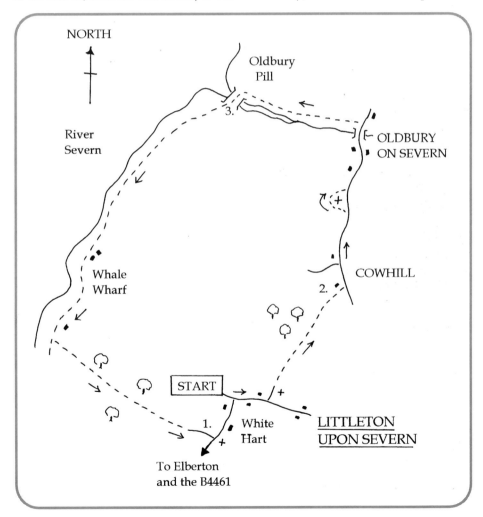

runs between two properties to join the road in Cowhill.

2 Turn left and follow this road for 350 yards to St Arilda's church. Bear left off of the road to cross a grassy area in front of the church, enter the churchyard and follow the path around the left-hand side of the church before rejoining the road. Turn left and follow the road down past Oldbury School to reach the Anchor

Oldbury Pill

Inn. Cross Oldbury Pill and immediately turn left to follow an access road towards Oldbury Sailing Club. In 300 yards, leave this road and walk across an open grassy area by Oldbury Pill to reach a sluice gate. Cross this sluice over the river, and join the embankment ahead – a flood defence – following the Severn downstream.

3 Follow these defences for 1¼ miles to reach a stile by a small inlet called Whale Wharf, just past some farm buildings on the left. Follow the flood defences beyond this stile for 600 yards to a footpath sign on the left below the embankment. This is at the far end of the third field on from

Whale Wharf. Drop down to a stile and footbridge, and follow the left edge of a field away from the river to its top left-hand corner. In this corner, pass through a gateway and follow an enclosed track for ¾ mile back to Littleton upon Severn where the track becomes a back lane. Follow this lane up to its junction with the main road in Littleton by a chapel, turn left and walk along the road for 150 yards back to the White Hart.

Date walk completed:

....

Places of Interest
Oldbury Nuclear Power Station has its own visitor centre, which is open from 10 am until 4 pm between March and October. Telephone: 01454 419899. At Severn Beach there is the **Severn Bridges Visitor Centre**, detailing the history of the two Severn crossings. The centre is signposted from junction 1 on the M48 motorway. Telephone: 01454 633511.

The Beaufort Arms

Distance: *4 miles*

OS Explorer 167 Thornbury, Dursley and Yate
GR 778870

A relatively gentle stroll, with the only significant climb being out of the Kilcott Valley up into Claypit Wood. Care needs to be exercised on the 350 yard stretch of road walk into Hawkesbury Upton towards journey's end where there is no pavement.

Starting point: The Hawkesbury Upton village hall car park, which lies just a few yards west of the Beaufort Arms on the opposite side of the road.

How to get there: Leave the main A46 at Dunkirk, midway between Bath and Stroud, and head in a westerly direction along the unclassified road for 1 mile to Hawkesbury Upton. Drive along the main street and, just past the Beaufort Arms, turn right into the village hall car park.

Hawkesbury Upton, with its many fine stone cottages and houses, lies high on the Cotswold plateau. To the west of the village, the hilltop drops away to the Severn Vale and an expansive view opens up towards the River Severn and the distant Welsh Hills. Dominating this outlook is the Somerset Monument, a lofty pinnacle that is a landmark for miles around. To the north of the village, the landscape falls away into the Kilcott Valley, one of those charming wooded valleys watered by a sparkling stream that are so characteristic of the Cotswold countryside. Here we find grand country residences all lovingly fashioned from that golden Cotswold limestone. The woodland paths above the valley are a delight in the spring, when traditional English flora forms a wonderful carpet of colour.

The **Beaufort Arms** is named after the Beaufort Family whose ancestral home was at the nearby Badminton Estate. Do not be misled by the exterior – inside this free house you will find a most traditional and welcoming pub atmosphere. The two bars both have low ceilings, and are decorated with a collection of brewery memorabilia as well as local prints and artefacts. The food on offer includes all of the usual pub favourites, whilst the Wickwar Brewery's Brand Oak Bitter and Weston's cider will certainly prove to be popular with drinkers in your party.

Opening times are 12 noon to 3 pm and 5.30 pm to 11 pm on Monday to Thursday; 12 noon to 11 pm on Friday and Saturday; 12 noon to 10.30 pm on Sunday.

Telephone: 01454 238217.

The Walk

1 Walk back along the main street to the green just past the Fox Inn, and bear left along a back lane signposted to Starveall. Follow this lane – called Back Street – for ¼ mile to a junction just outside Hawkesbury Upton. Turn right and follow a quiet lane that runs high above a valley on the left. In ½ mile cross a stile on the left to follow a public footpath, ignoring a slightly earlier footpath that passes through a handgate. Beyond the stile, follow a track across the top of the hillside. In 50 yards, where this track bears left downhill, cross a stile immediately ahead and follow a field boundary across the top of the hillside. At the far side of the field, bear left down to a stile in the end field boundary, just 15 yards down from the corner of the field. Cross the next field, keeping Bangel Wood on the left-hand side. At the far end of the field, cross a stile to join a lane.

2 Follow this lane ahead, passing through the hamlet of Upper Kilcott, and continue for another ½ mile down to the scattered collection of properties that make up Lower Kilcott. Turn left

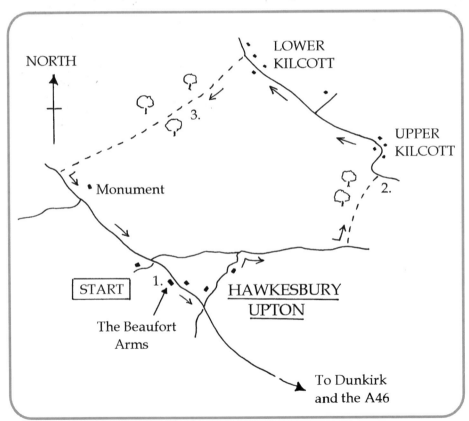

A tranquil scene in Hawkesbury Upton

opposite Mickley Cottage onto the Cotswold Way, and follow what is an unmetalled track uphill for 200 yards to a fork. Keep left, and climb on uphill to reach a gateway and open field. Walk ahead for 5 yards before passing through a gateway on the right into an adjoining field. Turn left and follow the top left edge of this field across to a gate and stile at the entrance to Claypit Wood.

3 Continue along the Cotswold Way as it passes through the woodland to reach a gate and stile and open field in 600 yards. Cross this stile, bear right and walk the whole length of the field ahead, making for a tin barn some 600 yards distant. Just by the barn, cross a stile and follow a

section of track along to the Hillesley to Hawkesbury Upton road. Turn left and follow this road for 350 yards with care up to the Somerset Monument, before walking along the pavement into Hawkesbury Upton to reach the village hall car park on the left.

Place of Interest

Horton Court, a National Trust property, lies just 3 miles from Hawkesbury Upton. For details, see Walk 13.

Date walk completed:

....

53

Exford

The White Horse Inn

L ying on the B3224, the main east–west route across Exmoor, it comes as no surprise to see horse boxes, Jeeps and a plethora of Countryside Alliance stickers around Exford, for this is a village famed for its connections with hunting and shooting, fishing and riding. The Devon & Somerset Staghounds, for example, have had their kennels in

Exford since 1875, whilst at one time no fewer that four blacksmiths operated out of the village. Houses and shops are grouped together around a pleasant village green, whilst at the western end of Exford the creeper-clad White Horse Inn sits alongside an ancient bridge over the River Exe. The village has a backdrop of small fields and hedgerows, a landscape that is so typical of this part of Exmoor and which can truly be appreciated from high on Room Hill. Below the hilltops lies the beautifully wooded Exe Valley, bringing a secluded and peaceful conclusion to this fine walk in one of England's magnificent National Parks.

Situated opposite the River Exe in the heart of Exford, the **White Horse Inn** is a lovely creeper-clad 16th century coaching inn. In the comfortable, beamed and carpeted bar there are country-themed prints adorning the walls, open log fires in winter, Exmoor Ale on tap, and an extensive menu listing traditional pub meals. Look out for the inn's specialities, namely venison, pheasant and partridge from the surrounding moors, locally caught lobster and daily deliveries of fresh fish, and the platter of Somerset cheeses – all from select local suppliers. There is also a Sunday lunch carvery.

Opening times: the White Horse is also a hotel and as such is open from 7.30 am until 11.30 pm each day. Food is served from 12 noon to 2.30 pm and 6 pm to 9.30 pm.

Telephone: 01643 831229.

Distance: *5 miles*

OS Outdoor Leisure 9 Exmoor
GR 854384

An energetic walk onto high Exmoor. The crossing of a ford over the River Exe may provide a challenge. Be sure to pack a towel to dry your feet!

Starting point: The village green in the centre of Exford.

How to get there: Lying on the B3224, Exford is to be found 6 miles west of Wheddon Cross en route to Simonsbath. Turn off northwards by the Crown Hotel and park alongside the village green. The White Horse Inn is 2 minutes walk along the B3224.

The Walk

1 From the green, follow the B3224 to the right in the direction of Simonsbath. Cross the River Exe by the White Horse Inn and turn left along the lane signposted to Withypool and Dulverton, initially passing the youth hostel. In 250 yards, on a sharp right-hand bend, turn left down the lane leading to Court Farm.

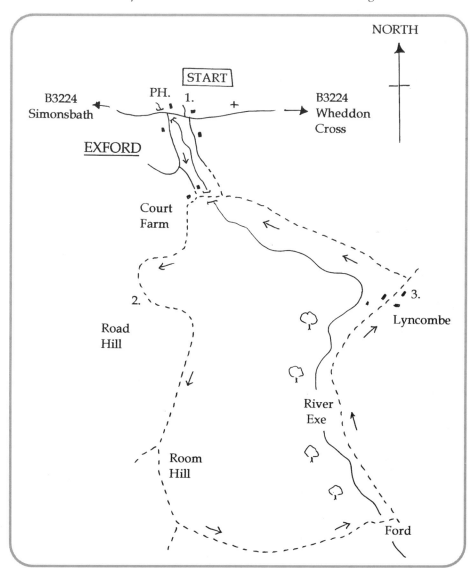

Follow this lane down through the farm and holiday complex, looking out for the waymarks to 'Withypool via Room Hill'. Having passed Court House and Court Mill, pass through a gateway ahead to follow a bridleway to Room Hill. Keep on what is an enclosed track for ½ mile until it eventually climbs to reach a gate at the top of Court Copse and an open hillside field.

❷ Cross this hillside field to a gateway opposite – with fine views to the left towards Exford – and, beyond this gateway, turn right and walk uphill to a gate at the end of a line of beech trees. Pass through this gateway, and follow the right edges of the next two fields before continuing along the bridleway as it crosses open moorland. In 200 yards, at a fork, bear left and continue for 500 yards to the next junction of paths. Keep on the left-hand path signposted to Winsford – passing the head of a combe on the left – and continue for 450 yards to a gate in the far corner of this open hilltop. Just before this gateway, turn left and walk downhill, keeping a beech hedgerow some 20 yards to the right. Drop steadily downhill for 650 yards to reach the River Exe, turn right for 50 yards and ford the river. Once across the River Exe, follow the path opposite that climbs to the right to reach a track. Turn left and follow this track across the side of the Exe Valley for 1 mile to reach a property called Lyncombe. Pass the house, barns and outbuildings to reach a gate and continue along the track for 20 yards to a stile and footpath on the left.

❸ Cross the stile, and bear right to follow a footpath across the field to a stile in the far corner by the River Exe.

The view looking towards Exford

Continue along a short section of riverside path to a pair of stiles, then cross the next riverside meadow to a gate in the end field boundary. Follow the right edge of the next field to a stile in the corner, then take the path across the following field that shortly bears right to cross to a stile in the corner of the field and a track. Turn left and follow this track back towards Exford. In 300 yards, just before the Exe and Court Farm, turn right through a kissing gate and follow a path alongside the river and across a meadow to reach a car park in Exford. Follow the road beyond the car park to the B3224, turn left and walk back to the village green.

Place of Interest

Tarr Steps, a prehistoric bridge carrying an ancient trackway across the River Barle, lies a few miles to the south of Exford. Dating from 1000 BC, some of the stones weigh 5 tons and were said to have been placed there by the Devil to win a bet.

Date walk completed:

....

The Rest & Be Thankful Inn

Thisexhilarating circuit takes you westwards from Dunkery Gate and returns over Dunkery Beacon, which, at 1,707 feet above the not too distant sea level, is the highest point on Exmoor. Refreshment awaits you a 2½ mile drive away at the characterful Rest &

Be Thankful Inn in Wheddon Cross. Dunkery's vast upland area is a plateau of ancient sandstone rocks that have been weathered and worn over millions of years by frosts, winds and rains. High ground always has a long tradition of human habitation, and this area proves no exception – the OS map reveals a proliferation of cairns, tumuli and barrows. The actual summit of Dunkery is strewn with the rough unhewn stones of ancient fire-hearths, and it is obviously as a 'beacon' in times of both danger and celebration that the lonely hilltop is best known. The Armada, for example, was signalled from here on 19th July 1588.

The **Rest & Be Thankful**, a former coaching inn, is located in Wheddon Cross, the highest village on Exmoor. There are welcoming log fires in winter. As for food, the delicious main courses might include roast duck with a tangy orange sauce or peppered pork served on long grain and wild rice, whilst the desserts range from sticky toffee pudding and chocolate fudge cake to blackberry and apple pie and cheeses. Being in the heart of the West Country, a glass of Tawny Bitter or Otter Ale should be an obligatory beverage with your meal!

Opening times are 11 am to 3 pm and 6.30 pm (7 pm in winter) to 11 pm every day.

Telephone: 01643 841222;
website: www.restandbethankful.co.uk

Distance: 5 miles

OS Outdoor Leisure 9 Exmoor
GR 897406

Rough tracks and byways that cross the open moorland of Exmoor

Starting point: The parking area at Dunkery Gate, immediately below the summit of Dunkery Beacon.

How to get there: The walk starts from Dunkery Gate, to the west of Wheddon Cross, a village that lies on the A396 Dunster to Tiverton road. From Wheddon Cross, follow the B3224 towards Exford for ¾ mile before following an unclassified lane signposted to Dunkery Beacon. In 1¾ miles, cross a cattle grid and park on the right-hand side of the road opposite a National Trust 'Dunkery Beacon' sign.

The Walk

1 Cross the road, and follow the bridlepath opposite, waymarked to Exford and Cloutsham. Follow this track for 2½ miles across the southern slopes of Dunkery until it reaches a quiet lane at Porlock Post. Turn right and follow the lane to the right – it is signposted to Cloutsham. Keep on this lane as it crosses the open moor – with views opening up towards the Bristol Channel – until a track goes off on the right in ¾ mile by a National Trust sign for Dunkery Beacon.

Striding out over the moorland

2 Turn right and follow a well-defined stony track up past a weather station on the left to reach Great Rowbarrow, a prehistoric cairn. Beyond this monument, bear left and follow the track across the hilltop for 1¼ miles to reach the summit of Dunkery Beacon, marked by an imposing cairn. Take the path to the right of the cairn, and walk downhill across the moor for ¾ mile to return to the car park at Dunkery Gate.

Date walk completed:

....

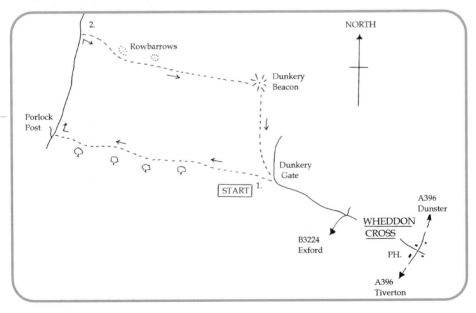

An ancient cairn on Dunkery

Places of Interest

Dunster lies just 8 miles north-east of Wheddon Cross. The medieval village, one of the beauty spots in the area, is best known for its castle, dramatically sited on a wooded hill. There is a sheltered terrace to the south on which tender plants and shrubs grow, and beautiful parkland in which to walk. **Dunster Castle** is home to the National Collection of Strawberry Trees and Britain's oldest lemon tree. Telephone: 01643 821314.

Porlock, cradled snugly in a glorious amphitheatre, lies a few miles north of Wheddon Cross. Set against a backdrop of Exmoor and its breathtaking uplands, the village looks out across the Bristol Channel towards Wales and the Welsh Hills. The visitor centre offers a range of services and displays, including a very good topographic map, and information about Porlock and Exmoor. It also houses a display of auroch (wild ox) bones dating from 1500 BC, which were recently found on the beach at Porlock Weir when exposed by tidal movement. Telephone: 01643 863150.

The Royal Oak Inn

simply that 'Ernest Bevin was born here'. Rising above the village, to a height of over 1,400 feet above sea level, is the heather and bracken clad hilltop of Winsford Hill. Perhaps more impressive is a massive chasm below it known as 'the Punchbowl'. There are – of course – legends attached to this natural amphitheatre, including one that talks of its creation by the Devil. In truth, it is a cirque basin formed by the power of glaciers during the Ice Age.

Considered by many experts to be 'Exmoor's most beautiful village', Winsford has no fewer than seven bridges that cross the Exe, ranging from the cobbled and amateurish to the strong, durable packhorse bridge. The village is perhaps best known around the world, however, for being the birthplace of politician Ernest Bevin. A tablet on a rather undistinguished residence states

The **Royal Oak Inn** was originally a farmhouse and dairy in the 12th century. With the starting of a wool trade and industry inland from the coast, packhorse carts stopped there for sustenance and the farmhouse developed into an overnight resting place. Today the Royal Oak – looking every bit the traditional inn under its canopy of thatch – is still situated opposite the village green with the Winn Brook running along at the front. The inn has expanded over the years and has been lovingly decorated and furnished providing comfortable and relaxing surroundings for its customers. A wide range of meals is offered, ranging from the more humble bar snack through to steaks and duck, guinea fowl and char-grilled chicken, fine meals that can be accompanied by fine real ales such as Cotleigh or Exmoor.

Distance: 4 miles

OS Outdoor Leisure 9 Exmoor
GR 906349

A challenging climb onto one of Exmoor's highest hilltops

Starting point: The parking area in the centre of Winsford.

How to get there: Turn off the A396 Dunster to Tiverton road at Coppleham Cross, 4 miles south of Wheddon Cross, taking the minor road signposted to Winsford. The parking area is alongside the crossroads in the centre of the village, just by the Bridge Cottage Tea Room.

Opening times are 11 am to 2.30 pm and 7 pm to 11 pm on Monday to Saturday; 12 noon to 3 pm and 7 pm to 11 pm on Sunday.

Telephone: 01643 851455.

The Walk

1 Return to the crossroads, and turn right along the road leading to Withypool. Follow this road through the local ford, past the church and on to a footpath on the left signposted to Winsford Hill, 100 yards past the last property on the left in the village. Pass through a gateway at this point, then continue ahead for 25 yards to a stile before following a tight enclosed path that runs below a property on the right to a stile. Continue along the left edge of the enclosure ahead to the next stile, before carrying on along another enclosed path that runs below an imposing property on the right. Continue to a gate and hillside field.

2 A succession of fields now have to be crossed! Follow the left edge of field 1 to a gate, before crossing field 2 to the right-hand of a pair of gateways opposite. Follow the left edges of fields 3 and 4, then pass to the right of an outbuilding in field 5 to reach a gateway. In field 6, cross to the right-hand of two gateways opposite and walk along the left edge of field 7 to reach a farm road. Follow this road down to Withycombe Farm and continue along the track that bears left to run between two barns before dropping downhill to cross a stream. Beyond this stream, head uphill to a pair of gateways.

3 Pass through the left-hand gateway and follow a fieldpath around the right edge of the field ahead as it climbs towards the Punchbowl. As the path levels out, turn right through a gateway then left up past some beech trees to reach a gate at the top of the field and the open moorland. Follow the grassy ride ahead for 150 yards to a fork, and keep left to

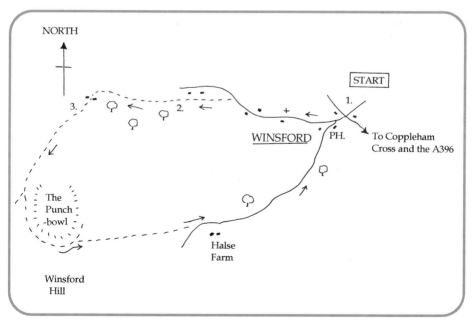

The Punchbowl

follow the path around the western edge of the Punchbowl before bearing left to pass around its head. Do not continue around the far side of this natural feature – instead keep ahead along the grassy ride heading away from the Punchbowl across Winsford Hill, ignoring all side turns. Stay on the path as it eventually drops downhill to a lane and cattle grid by Halse Farm. Turn left and follow this lane for 1 mile to the Royal Oak in Winsford. Turn right at the junction beyond the inn to return to the crossroads in the village.

Date walk completed:

....

Place of Interest

The **National Park visitor centre** at Dulverton, 6 miles south of Winsford, houses exhibitions about the heritage of Dulverton and the importance of the surrounding woodlands, as well as an art gallery and library. It is located in the main square in the town, adjacent to a large public car park and a variety of shops and services. Telephone: 01398 323841; website: www.exmoor-nationalpark.gov.uk

Kilve 19

The Hood Arms

local shale is oil-bearing, and Kilve had aspirations in the 1920s to become the Dallas of Somerset! In earlier times, there was a chantry in the village, and to this day its ivy-clad ruins adorn the roadside just below the church. It was destroyed by fire in 1850, and the emerald and blue colouration of the flames confirmed local suspicions that here was a hotbed of liquor smuggling. The oil magnates and the smugglers have long-since gone, leaving a peaceful corner of Somerset for today's walkers to explore and enjoy.

Few travellers heading across West Somerset venture north of the main Minehead road to explore the coastline east of Watchet. This is an intriguing landscape with clifftop paths, crumbling rock faces, pebbly beaches and more than a little sense of history. The

The **Hood Arms** is a traditional 17th century coaching inn, offering excellent food, good service and a warm welcome. It lies at the foot of the Quantock Hills, and boasts a delightful walled garden where walkers and cyclists can take a break from their exertions. The menu offers such selections as sea bass fillet steak, Jack Daniels chicken and a local Somerset pork dish, based upon cider rather than whisky! Nelson described Samuel, Admiral Hood as 'the best officer that England can boast of'. Born in Somerset, it seems wholly appropriate that an inn so close to the sea should bear his illustrious name.

Distance: 6 miles

OS Explorer 140 Quantock Hills and Bridgwater
GR 149429

Tracks, quiet lanes and footpaths crossing the undulating landscape that borders the West Somerset coast

Starting point: The car park opposite the Hood Arms in Kilve.

How to get there: Kilve lies on the A39 Minehead road, 10 miles from Bridgwater. Just past the Hood Arms - on the opposite side of the road - there is a public car park that is also used by the inn's customers.

Opening times are 12 noon to 2 pm and 6 pm to 11 pm on Monday to Saturday; 12 noon to 3 pm and 7 pm to 10.30 pm on Sunday.

Telephone: 01278 741210.

The Walk

1 Exit the car park, turn right along the A39 past the Hood Arms and, in 150 yards, by a red telephone box, fork left along an enclosed bridleway that runs behind a property. Follow this track uphill for 600 yards to its junction with a lane, turn left and, in 50 yards, right along a cul-de-sac lane that leads to Lower Hill Farm. In 400 yards, when this lane reaches the farm, keep ahead along a track that runs to the right of the farmhouse and up to a gateway. Continue along the right edges of the next two fields and walk across a third field – bearing slightly left all the while – to a gate and lane in Kilton.

2 Follow the lane to the left for 400 yards and, just past West Kilton Farm, pass through a gate in the hedge on the left and cross the field ahead to a stile and Kilton church. Walk to the right through the churchyard to rejoin the lane, turn left and continue for ½ mile to a track on the right leading to Lilstock's redundant church, ignoring a right turn along the way. Continue past this track and on through Lilstock for 250 yards and, just past Lilstock Farm, where the lane bears sharply to the right, turn left along the track that leads through to the parking area for Lilstock Beach. Continue past the parking area to reach the coast itself. Follow the coast path to the left for 2 miles before passing through a wooden handgate to reach the shoreline at Kilve.

3 At this point, turn left and follow a

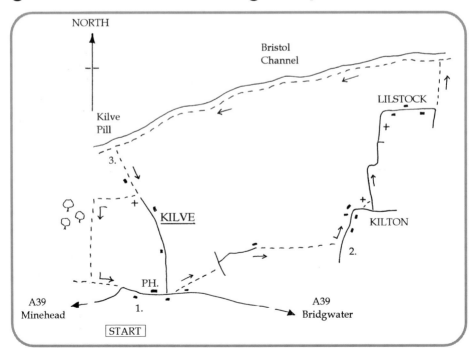

The ruins of the chantry at Kilve

track – it becomes a lane – inland for ¼ mile to reach Kilve church. Pass through the churchyard to reach a handgate just beyond the church, and turn right down to a track. Follow this track to the left across 2 fields to reach the northern end of East Wood. Turn left and, keeping the wood on your right, head uphill across two fields bordering the woodland. Pass through a gap in the hedge at the end of the second field, turn right through a handgate into the adjoining field and turn left to follow the left edge of a field for 350 yards to a gateway in its corner.

Halfway across the next field, cross a stile in the hedge on the left and walk across to the far right corner of a paddock to reach a gate and the main A39. Follow this road to the left *with care* into Kilve and, just past a sign indicating a car park, follow a gravelled path on the right, running parallel to the main road, that leads back to the car park.

Date walk completed:

....

Place of Interest

Hinkley Point Power Station lies just a few miles east of Kilve on the Somerset coast. Free tours of the complex begin at the visitor centre, where hands-on displays explain how electricity is created. A minibus takes you off to the power station to see the real life workings of a nuclear plant. The area around Hinkley Point includes Sites of Special Scientific Interest, managed in conjunction with English Nature. Nightingales, for example, find the habitats particularly appealing. Telephone 01278 654334 for more details, especially regarding the tours of the actual site.

Triscombe
The Blue Ball Inn

The Quantock Hills comprise a well-wooded ridge that runs in a north-westerly direction from Taunton and Bridgwater to the Bristol Channel coast at West Quantockhead. The woodlands are predominantly of oak and are rich in typical woodland birds, especially woodpeckers and redstarts, whilst buzzards are often seen circling high overhead on rising currents of warm air. Other wildlife habitats include areas of open heathland and sheltered combes, where red deer can sometimes be seen. Along the way, our steps pass the Triscombe Stone, marking the meeting point of a series of drove tracks, as well as the trig point at Wills Neck, at 1,275 feet above sea level the highest point on the Quantocks. The views from this lofty hilltop perch extend towards Minehead and the Bristol Channel, as well as deep into Exmoor. A fine upland walk across some of the finest landscape that Somerset can offer.

The **Blue Ball Inn** is a picturesque sandstone and thatch hostelry – formerly traditional coaching stables – that nestles at the foot of the Quantock Hills. The long, low building slopes gently downwards on three levels, and has been imaginatively divided into seating areas by hand-cut beech partitions, employing local craft skills. The imaginative menu might typically include Thai curries or lemon and thyme risotto, cod in beer batter or pasta with garlic and rosemary sauce. Lunchtime also sees lighter options such as sandwiches and filled rolls. As well as a fine selection of wines, the Blue Ball also offers real ales such as Otter Ale and Cotleigh Tawny.

Opening times are 12 noon to 3 pm and 7 pm to 11 pm every day, also all afternoon during August.

Telephone: 01984 618242.

Distance: *5 miles*

OS Explorer 140 Quantock Hills and Bridgwater
GR 155355

Quiet lanes and tracks, with steep slopes along the way. The descent from the hills at the end of the walk is extremely steep – details of an alternative easier route have also been given!

Starting point: The Blue Ball Inn at Triscombe.

How to get there: Turn off the A358 Minehead road 8 miles north-west of Taunton, on an unclassified road signposted to Triscombe. Follow this lane for 1 mile to reach the Blue Ball. There is room for careful roadside parking around the inn.

The Walk

1 Follow the lane opposite the Blue Ball, waymarked with a Quantock Greenway signpost. In 1 mile, where this lane bears left by Little Quantock Farm, turn right through a gate and follow a track up past a stable block and uphill through Little Quantock Combe towards the Quantock hilltops. Some 600 yards on from the road, pass through a gate on the left to enter the open hilltops. Follow the wide grassy path ahead, steadily climbing uphill and, in 400 yards, when this path reaches an area of bracken and gorse, bear right and continue along the path to reach a belt of beech trees. Join a track by these trees, turn left and walk past a pond to reach a gate and lane at Crowcombe Gate.

2 Turn right across a cattle grid and, in

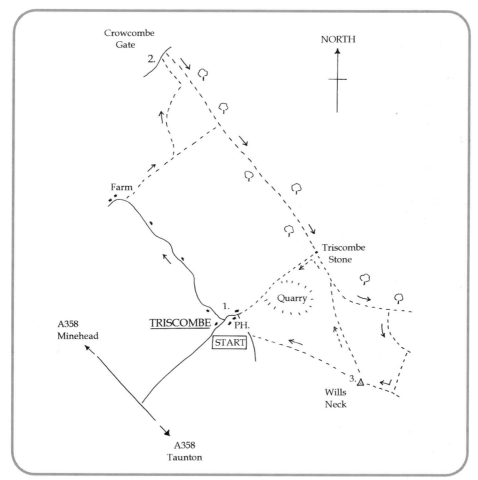

75 yards, turn right along a wide sandstone track. Follow the main track ahead for 1¼ miles, ignoring all side turnings, until it reaches the Triscombe Stone with its car park on the left. Continue ahead along the track for 600 yards to a point where a track goes off sharply on the right, just before an area of open ground high above a combe. Turn right and follow this track around the head of the combe – Aisholt Common. In 350 yards, fork right along a side track and climb uphill for 150 yards to a junction on the hilltop. Turn right and walk ahead to the trig point at Wills Neck.

❸ There are two routes back to the Blue Ball. For the harder route, take the path that passes to the left of the trig point and continue across the hilltop for 600 yards before dropping very steeply downhill through woodland to reach a stile and track. Cross this track, and continue downhill on a rough, steep path to reach a lane in 100 yards. Turn right to a road junction and the Blue Ball Inn. For an

A woodland path in the Quantocks

easier walk, which adds no more than 600 yards to the walk, take the path that passes to the right of the trig point and head across the hilltop to return to the track followed earlier in the walk. Follow this track to the left back to the Triscombe Stone, before turning left over a cattle grid to walk along a rutted and pot-holed road downhill for ½ mile to the inn.

Date walk completed:
....

Places of Interest

Crowcombe Heathfield Station on the **West Somerset Railway** lies just 2 miles south-west of the Blue Ball Inn. The railway has all the atmosphere of a Great Western Railway branch line. There are ten restored stations along the route, each having its own charm and character. Many have signalboxes, engine sheds, museums, displays, steam engines and other rolling stock to see. From Bishops Lydeard, trains run beside the Quantock Hills northwards to the coast of the Bristol Channel – locally called the 'Severn Sea' – at Watchet and Blue Anchor. The end of the line is the holiday town of **Minehead**, with its sandy beach, thrilling fun fair, beautiful gardens and lots of shops to explore. For further information on this preserved steam railway, telephone 01643 704996; website: www.west-somerset-railway.co.uk

To the south-east of Triscombe and 6 miles north of Taunton, **Fyne Court** in Broomfield is a visitor centre for the Quantocks as well as the headquarters of the Somerset Wildlife Trust. The Court was at one time the home of Andrew Crosse, the pioneer electrical scientist. Telephone 01823 451587 for full details of opening times and all of the special events and exhibitions held here.

The Anchor Inn

A unique landscape, wide open vistas and big skies all combine in this memorable coastal excursion. Combwich has been likened to a Dutch settlement on account of its watery environment, low-lying land and small vessels that moor along the local inlet, a shelter from the treacherous waters of the Parrett Estuary that quite literally runs up against the village. The Parrett itself, with its source in the springs around Cheddington in Dorset, is one of Somerset's great rivers. Downstream of Combwich, the Parrett flows into Bridgwater Bay and the Severn Estuary and it is here that we find one of Britain's great nature reserves – the Bridgwater Bay National Nature Reserve. A wild and desolate coastal path brings the walk around to the sand dunes and beach at Steart – whose westerly outlook encompasses much of the South Wales coast – before a level fieldpath returns the visitor to the River Parrett and Combwich.

The **Anchor Inn**, as befits its name, resembles in part a twin-funnelled paddle steamer. Overlooking the River Parrett, its waterside location is only fully appreciated from the inn's first floor terrace. As well as a main bar and snug, the Anchor also boasts a lawned beer garden for those warm summer days. The fine home-cooked food includes sandwiches, rolls and salads, as well as steaks, chicken, pork and lamb dishes, together with seafood and vegetarian options. Fine real ales and ciders are also available, as well as teas and coffees.

Summer opening times are 12 noon to 11 pm on Monday to Friday; 11 am to 11 pm on Saturday; 12 noon to 10.30 pm on Sunday. **Winter opening times** *are 12 noon to 2.30 pm and 6.30 pm to 11 pm on Tuesday to Friday (closed on Monday); 12 noon to 11 pm on Saturday; 12 noon to 10.30 pm on Sunday.*

Telephone: 01278 653612.

Distance: *7 miles*

OS Explorer 140 Quantock Hills and Bridgwater
GR 260424

Level flood defences, coastal paths and fieldpaths in and around Bridgwater Bay

Starting point: The Anchor Inn at Combwich.

How to get there: Turn off the A39 Minehead road 4 miles west of Bridgwater, following the signs for Combwich and Cannington. Continue into Combwich, bearing left up Church Hill and then right down Ship Lane before parking on the roadside opposite the Anchor Inn by a children's play area alongside the river.

The Walk

1 Cross the grass by the play area to reach the banks of the River Parrett. Follow the riverbank downstream for 1¾ miles to a point where a well-defined track bears off on the left away from the riverbank, some 600 yards beyond a pond on the right. Follow this track for just over 1 mile to the lane in Steart. Turn right and follow this lane for 400 yards to a gateway, before continuing along an unmetalled track towards Steart Point. In 200 yards, keep on the track as it bears right and, in another 50 yards, turn left up a side track leading up to the Bridgwater Bay Reserve. Some 2,560 hectares in extent, this consists largely of intertidal mudflats, sandflats and shingle ridges. Internationally and nationally important numbers of wintering and passage waders and wildfowl occur, whilst shelduck moult within the bay and widgeon graze on the saltmarsh. A recently erected tower

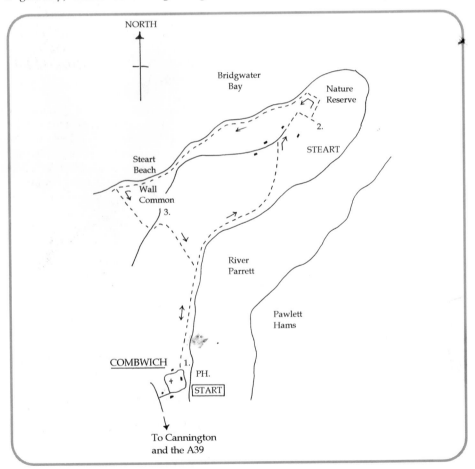

NORTH

Bridgwater Bay

Nature Reserve

2.

STEART

Steart Beach

Wall Common

3.

River Parrett

Pawlett Hams

COMBWICH   1.

PH.

START

To Cannington and the A39

provides excellent views across the whole of the reserve, and a number of hides offer vantage points across the mouth of the Parrett.

2 Walk ahead across the reserve for 50 yards, then cross a stile on the left to join a coast path, making the obvious detours to explore the various hides first. Follow the coast path in a southerly direction for 1¼ miles until it reaches a gateway just north of Steart Beach.

The inlet at Combwich

Cross the grassy area and dunes ahead to reach a red brick structure on the beach, before following the foreshore – or the track immediately behind the foreshore – for ½ mile across the northern edge of Wall Common. On the far side of Wall Common, turn left – walking away from the coast – and follow a raised embankment across the southern boundary of the common to reach the lane running from Stockland Bristol to Steart.

3 Cross this lane, and follow the track opposite as it bears left down to two gateways. Pass through the gateway on the right, and walk ahead across what appears to be a long thin field. In 300 yards, where this field widens, walk over to a gateway almost in the far right corner of the field. Cross to a gateway in the far right corner of the next field, before rejoining the banks of the River Parrett. Turn right and retrace your steps for 1 mile back into Combwich.

Date walk completed:

....

Place of Interest

Bridgwater, just a few miles south of Combwich, was the birthplace of Admiral Blake. The **Admiral Blake Museum** occupies the house that is reputedly the great man's birthplace. Born in 1598, Blake was Cromwell's General-at-Sea, and the Blake Room in the museum contains personal effects such as the Admiral's sea chest and letters. The museum also houses displays relating to the Monmouth Rebellion, including a diorama of the Battle of Sedgemoor, the last battle fought on English soil. Other exhibits explore the archaeology of the area as well as the industrial history of Bridgwater. Telephone: 01278 456127.

This walk is centred upon the quiet north-eastern corner of the Taunton Deane area and two lesser-known waterways – the River Tone and the Bridgwater & Taunton Canal. The Tone was navigable as far as Ham Mills until the 1920s, although the opening of the canal in 1827 did lead to a dramatic reduction in river-borne traffic. Today, both waterways lie in quiet isolation, separated from the rest of Britain's canal network and little known as a result. What remains is a secluded watery paradise, well away from the main tourist trail.

The Riverside Tavern – originally the New Inn – lies just above the River Tone in Creech St Michael. Standing next door to the village church, the pub was actually built on the foundations of the old Church House run by the monks of Montacute. Perhaps best known for its Sunday roasts, an à la carte menu is also available, as well as a variety of other dishes ranging from snacks to mixed grills. On warm summer days, the perfect place to sit is in front of the Riverside Tavern, overlooking the inn's pretty garden.

Opening times are *11.30 am to 2.30 pm and 6 pm to 11 pm every day.*

Telephone: 01823 442257.

Distance: *5 miles*

OS Explorer 128 Taunton and the Blackdown Hills
GR 275255

A flat walk along riverside paths, canal towpath and drove tracks

Starting point: The picnic area and car park by the Bridgwater & Taunton Canal in Creech St Michael.

How to get there: Turn off the A361 Taunton to Glastonbury road just 600 yards east of its junction with the A38 north of Taunton, taking the unclassified road signposted to Creech St Michael. In 2 miles, on a sharp right bend in the village just before the road crosses the River Tone, turn left into Bull Street. Almost immediately, turn left into Vicarage Lane and follow this back lane around to a car park by the Bridgwater & Taunton Canal.

The Walk

1 Retrace your steps back down to Bull Street, turn left and follow this road past the church and Riverside Tavern and on for 400 yards to where it becomes a private road. At this point, cross a stile on the right and follow the banks of the River Tone downstream for ¾ mile to a footbridge. Cross the river, walk down to the lane in Ham and turn left. In 350 yards, where the lane bears right by Old Ham Wharf Farm, rejoin the Tone by a suspension bridge and follow the riverside track ahead for ½ mile until it ends at a gateway.

2 At this point, turn right along a track – Westmoor Drove – and follow it for just over ½ mile to its junction with another track. Turn left and walk along to Knapp Bridge and the Tone. Cross the river and, immediately, go over a stile on the left into a meadow. Follow the river upstream across five fields until, in ½ mile, part way across the fifth field, the path bears right away from the river. Keep following the left edge of this field until it reaches a track just before a railway line, with a gateway on the left. Follow the track beyond this gate to a bridge, cross the railway line and continue ahead for 100 yards to reach the Bridgwater & Taunton

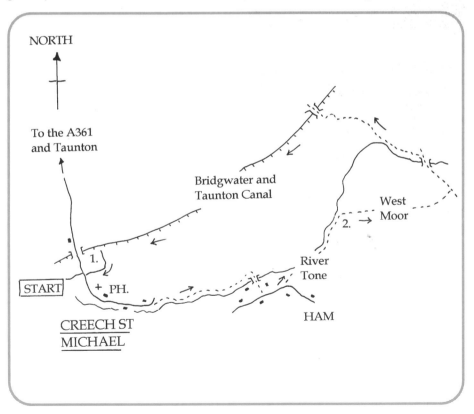

NORTH

To the A361
and Taunton

Bridgwater and
Taunton Canal

West
Moor

2.

River
Tone

START   + PH.

1.

HAM

CREECH ST
MICHAEL

The Bridgwater & Taunton Canal

Canal. Follow the canal to the left for almost 1½ miles back to the canalside car park in Creech.

Date walk completed:

....

Place of Interest

The **Willow and Wetlands Visitor Centre** at Stoke St Gregory, just north-east of Creech St Michael, is owned and run by the Coate family, who have been growing willow on the Somerset Levels since 1819. Visitors will find displays that relate to the ancient art of willow growing and basket-making in this corner of the Levels. Telephone 01823 490249 for more information. The centre does not open on Sundays.

The Sedgemoor Inn

The flat and lonely fields to the north of Westonzoyland were the site of the Battle of Sedgemoor, the last battle to be fought on English soil. This was an attempt by the Western Rebellion, an ill-equipped and untrained army of peasants, to overthrow King Charles II's brother James. This walk explores the battlefield site, as well as a network of drove tracks, some of which were undoubtedly used by the rebel army to reach Westonzoyland from Bridgwater. On those cold autumnal mornings when the mists envelop Sedgemoor, the imaginative mind can easily recreate the scene of 6th July 1685. The ghostly shapes in the distance – in all probability nothing more than a herd of Friesian cows – could well be Monmouth's rebels stealing across the moors under cover of darkness!

The **Sedgemoor Inn**, whitewashed and creeper covered, has a colourful sign that depicts the events of the Battle of Sedgemoor. The inn – the Royalist base before the battle itself – also boasts an interesting collection of related memorabilia, including Monmouth's declaration of his illegitimacy. Offering good value, traditional pub food, the Sedgemoor Inn also serves fine real ales that might include Oakhill Mendip Gold and Marston's Pedigree.

Opening times are from 11.30 am to 11 pm every day.

Telephone: 01278 691382.

Distance: *6 miles*

OS Explorer 140 Quantock Hills and Bridgwater
GR 352347

Fieldpaths and drove tracks that cross a level landscape

Starting point: Westonzoyland church, a short distance along the road from the Sedgemoor Inn.

How to get there: Westonzoyland lies 4 miles east of Bridgwater, on the A372. Cars can be left on the roadside near the church although, as this is a main road, you may prefer to park on one of the side roads around the village.

The Walk

1 Follow the A372 towards Bridgwater to a point 100 yards beyond the edge of Westonzoyland where an unmarked track goes off on the right. This last 100 yards has narrow grass verges but no pavements – take great care! Turn right and, in 600 yards, just past a telegraph pole on the right and 40 yards before a right-hand bend, pass through a gateway and follow the left edge of the field ahead. In the

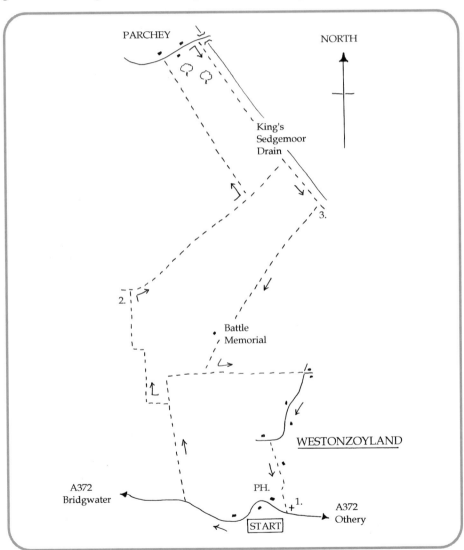

corner of the field, pass through a gap in the hedge, turn right and walk up to the top corner of the field where the path reaches Chedzoy New Cut. Turn left to a bridge, cross the Cut and follow the right edge of the field ahead to a gate in the corner and a track.

2 Join this track – Moor Drove – and follow it to the right for ¾ mile until it reaches a prominent junction where a track goes off on the left, passing through occasional gateways along the way and ignoring all side turns. Follow this track for ¾ mile to the lane in Parchey and turn right. In 350 yards, just before Parchey Bridge and King's Sedgemoor Drain, turn right through a gateway and follow a grassy track into some woodland. Keep on this track – it soon bears left – to reach a gate and meadow by the Drain. Follow the bank of the Drain to the right for 1 mile, crossing eight fields. At the far side of the final field, just before a series of electricity power lines, turn right away from the Drain to a gate and a track called Langmoor Drove.

3 Follow this track in a southerly direction for ¾ mile to its junction with another track, passing the Battle of

The monument commemorating the Battle of Sedgemoor

Sedgemoor monument just before the junction. Turn left and follow a track for 500 yards to Bussex Farm. Turn right and follow Monmouth Road for 500 yards as it winds its way into Westonzoyland. Having passed Bussex Square on the right, continue to a tarmac footpath on the left just before a left turn called Monmouth Close. Follow this tarmac path back to Westonzoyland church and the A372, keeping right at a junction by some bungalows along the way.

Date walk completed:

. . . .

Place of Interest

Westonzoyland is the home of **Somerset's earliest steam-powered pumping station**, built in 1830. It is to be found beside the River Parrett, south of the A372. Once a hard-working guardian of the flatlands, it is now a museum displaying stationary steam engines and exhibits of land drainage history. Pride of place goes to the station's pumping engine, the Easton and Amos. It is still in the main engine house, built in 1861 to replace an earlier engine that had been carrying out the pumping work since 1831. Other exhibits include a Wills engine, a Lancashire boiler, the original forge and a Lister diesel generating plant, to name just a few. The pumping station is open periodically to visitors. Visit www.wzlet.org or telephone 01275 472385 to find out details of opening times and dates.

Long Sutton
The Devonshire Angel

In much of the British Isles, the word 'moor' is used to denote a tract of uncultivated upland, in the West Country perhaps most famously associated with Exmoor and Dartmoor. Not so in South Somerset! Here the moors are the areas of flat, low-lying land that

Distance: 6 miles

OS Explorer 129 Yeovil and Sherborne
GR 469254

Other than a climb onto Knole Hill, this walk explores what has been described as 'an excessively horizontal landscape'

Starting point: The Devonshire Angel in Long Sutton.

How to get there: Approaching via the A303, leave at the Podimore Roundabout and follow the A372 towards Langport for 4 miles to Long Sutton, before taking the left turn along the B3165 into the village centre. Turn left immediately past the Devonshire Angel and park in Cross Lane by the inn.

were in centuries past quite literally inland seas, marshland or bog. South of Long Sutton and Knole we find King's Moor, Little Moor and Rod Moor, extensive areas of lowland drained by the River Yeo and an associated network of rhynes – the local name for drainage ditches. The moors are a unique habitat, attracting a rich array of wildfowl. Long Sutton itself is a pretty enough place, with its fine church tower, whilst Knole boasts a splendid hillock that brings far-ranging views across the local moors. This fine walk provides a perfect introduction to a little-explored corner of Somerset's lowlands.

The **Devonshire Angel**, a former 17th century hunting lodge, overlooks an idyllic village green. The lunchtime menu ranges from baps – with a variety of delicious fillings – through to traditional fare such as fishcakes and bangers and mash, whilst the evening menu represents some of the best of modern cooking. There are no fewer than eight Belgian beers on tap, and cider lovers will welcome such fine options as Old Rosie and Stowford Press. The publicity material states that 'there is nothing quite like the Devonshire Angel around' and for once this is no mere hype!

Opening times are 12 noon to 3 pm and 6 pm to 11 pm on Monday to Saturday; 12 noon to 4 pm on Sunday.

Telephone: 01458 241271;
website: www.devonshireangel.com

The Walk

1 Follow Cross Lane away from the Devonshire Arms for 350 yards to a junction by a small green, turn left and, in 50 yards, turn right along an unmarked track. Follow this track for 450 yards to a footpath on the left signposted to Knole. Follow this path – it is effectively a track – for 200 yards to a gate, then follow the left edge of a field alongside a barn to a stile in the corner of the field. Follow the left edge of the next field to a stile in the corner and, in the following field, walk ahead along the northern flanks of Knole Hill for 40 yards to a stile on the left. Beyond this stile, bear half-right and cross to a stile in the far right corner of the field ahead before continuing down an enclosed path to the road in Knole.

2 Turn right, walk through Knole and, where the lane bears left, cross a stile on the right and follow an enclosed path alongside Mill Cottage to a handgate and hillside field below Knole Hill. Head straight uphill and, on the hilltop, bear right to reach a flagpole on the summit. Continue beyond this flagpole to a pair of handgates at the western end of the hilltop enclosure. Enter a hilltop field, bear left downhill and make for a stile in the bottom right corner of the field. Follow the right edge of the next field to a stile in the corner and join a track. Turn left and, in just 50 yards, turn right along a track called Driveway Drove. Follow this track in a southerly direction for ¾ mile to its junction with Kingsmoor Drove. Cross a footbridge directly ahead over a drainage channel to a stile, before crossing the field in front of you to reach a footbridge over the River Yeo.

3 Cross the river, and bear right to a gate and field bordering the Yeo. Cross

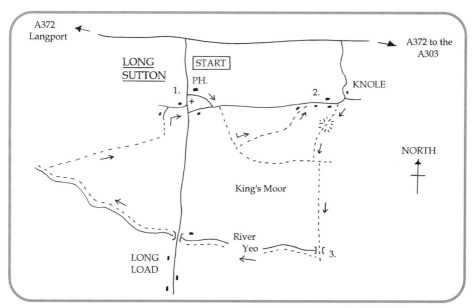

Looking towards Knole

the top of this field to a gateway opposite, with the Yeo on the right. Walk ahead for a few yards to another old gateway, before continuing ahead along the overgrown riverbank. Follow the river downstream for 1 mile, through gateways along the way, until the path reaches Long Load Pumping Station. Walk past the pumping station to a handgate, before continuing along a track to reach the B3165. Turn right, cross Load Bridge and immediately go over a stile on the left to join the riverbank alongside the Yeo. Follow the riverbank downstream across four fields for 1 mile. At the far side of the

fourth field, turn right away from the river down to a gate, enter a field and follow a drainage ditch on the left across to a gate in the far left corner of the field. Beyond this gate, follow Withmoor Drove back into Long Sutton. On the edge of the village, keep on this lane as it bears left, walk past Brook Farm and continue to a junction. Turn right to reach the B3165 before turning left back up to the Devonshire Arms.

Date walk completed:

....

Places of Interest

The ancient town of **Somerton** lies just to the north of Long Sutton and offers visitors a market place with a battlemented 17th century cross, an old Town Hall and a plethora of Georgian houses.

To the west of Long Sutton, **Langport** boasts the houses of wealthy merchants of yesteryear, for here was 19th century opulence. Just south of Langport is **Muchelney**, with the remains of a Benedictine Abbey and a surviving Priest's House. With such a wealth of interest, be sure to visit the **River Parrett Visitor Centre** in Langport. The centre provides an opportunity to discover life on the Somerset Levels and moors, one of lowland Britain's most unchanged landscapes. Telephone: 01458 250350.

The King's Arms Inn

M ontacute, deep in the South Somerset countryside, is best known for its grand mansion – now a noted National Trust property. Montacute House and the surrounding villages are all lovingly crafted from the

warm honey-coloured Ham stone. These days Ham Hill, site of the stone quarries, is a delightful Country Park covering 154 acres of woodland and grassland, where quarrying and the construction of fortifications have left a network of ramparts, ridges and terraces. The panoramic views from this lofty hilltop perch encompass the Mendip and Quantock Hills, as well as the Dorset Downs to the south. Another viewpoint is the 18th century lookout tower high on St Michael's Hill. The hilltop, itself part of the Montacute Estate, was formerly the site of a Norman Castle. A truly memorable walk of literal highpoints!

The **King's Arms Inn** is a charming country house crafted from the local Ham stone. As well as cask-conditioned ales and fine wines, visitors can enjoy seasonal home-cooked English cuisine in either the Cottage Restaurant or the Abbey Room. The choices range from bar snacks right through to romantic à la carte dining, which ensures that every conceivable taste is catered for. For those warm, balmy summer days, this fine hostelry can also offer a delightful garden, quite the perfect place to relax after a stroll on the South Somerset hills. If your taste is for the cup that 'cheers but doth not inebriate', then the King's Arms can also offer morning coffee and afternoon tea.

Opening times are 11 am to 11 pm every day.

Telephone: 01935 822513.

Distance: *5 miles*

OS Explorer 129 Yeovil and Sherborne GR 497170

A climb from Montacute onto Ham Hill, followed by a descent back into the village. An optional ascent of St Michael's Hill provides the stiffest ascent along the way!

Starting point: The King's Arms Inn in Montacute.

How to get there: Travelling on the A303, turn off 3 miles south-west of Ilchester and follow the A3088 road signposted to Yeovil. In just 1 mile, leave this main road to follow the unclassified road signposted to Montacute. On entering the village, park on the roadside in the vicinity of the King's Arms Inn.

The Walk

1 Follow the side lane alongside the King's Arms, which passes up between the church and former village school. At the top of this lane, by Abbey Farm, walk along the gravelled track ahead signposted as a private road. Having passed a converted farm building, continue along a track that passes through two gateways before continuing as a grassy ride up to a gate and Hollow Lane. Turn right for just a few yards before passing through a handgate on the right into a hillside field. Turn left and follow the top left edges of the next three fields to a pair of handgates and a lane just beyond a stable block. Join the road, turn right and, in 150 yards, pass through a handgate on the left just past a farm complex. Turn right and climb the bank ahead up to a gate and fence running

across an open hilltop. Follow the line of the fence – with the fence on the right – across the hilltop for 400 yards to a gate. Beyond the gate, turn left and walk all of the way around the perimeter of a hilltop field to a gate in the far right corner just by a lane at the entrance to the Ham Hill Country Park.

2 Pass through the gateway, turn right and, just before the road, turn left along an enclosed woodland path. Follow this path down to a bungalow on the right called Hill Top and the entrance to a quarry on the left. Walk straight ahead past the quarry entrance, continue through the woodland and out onto an open clearing. Cross this clearing, follow the path opposite back into woodland and continue for 100 yards to a junction with a well-defined track on the western edge of Ham Hill. Follow this path to the right

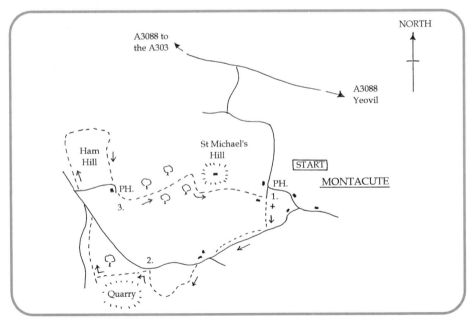

for 300 yards to reach Norton car park, then bear right out to the lane running across Ham Hill. Turn left and follow this lane along to a road junction. Continue ahead past a car park and viewpoint and, in 100 yards, turn right along a side turning signposted to the Prince of Wales. In 30 yards, pass through a handgate on the left and follow a gravelled path to the northern end of Ham Hill. Climb the embankment up to a war memorial, and turn right to follow the hilltop embankments around the northern and eastern edges of Ham Hill for ½ mile to a handgate and the car park for the Prince of Wales pub.

The war memorial atop Ham Hill

❸ Turn left alongside the pub to follow a stepped path downhill from the lane, signposted to Montacute. At the bottom of these steps, pass through a handgate on the left to follow another stepped path, signposted to East Stoke. At the bottom of these steps, turn right through a gateway and shortly, at the next junction, follow the bridleway ahead, signposted to Montacute. Follow the main track ahead for ¾ mile through Hedgecock Hill Wood – ignoring all side turns – to where the track bears sharply to the left and drops downhill. At this point, turn right and follow a track along the eastern end of the woodland. In 200 yards, turn left down a side path and drop down to a stile and an open field – ahead are the wooded slopes of St Michael's Hill. Walk across the field, passing to the right of St Michael's Hill, to reach the south-eastern corner of this isolated hillock. (A stile in the fence on the left gives access to a steep path that climbs to the tower at the summit of St Michael's Hill.) On reaching the corner of this wooded hill, follow a sunken path downhill between trees – walking away from St Michael's Hill – down to a gateway. Walk down past Abbey Farm to another gate, turn left and follow the lane back to the King's Arms.

Date walk completed:
....

Places of Interest
Montacute House (NT), built in the late 16th century for Sir Edward Phelps - Speaker of the House of Commons under James I - is a true stately home. Elegant chimneys, carved parapets, splendid staterooms and formal gardens combine to form what is a nationally renowned masterpiece. Telephone 01935 823289 for details of opening times for the house and garden.

The Fleet Air Arm Museum at Yeovilton lies just a few miles north-east of Montacute. Four display halls portray the development of naval aviation from the First World War to the Gulf War. Telephone: 01935 840565; website: www.fleetairarm.com

The Red Lion

cliff-like, to the sea of the central plain. Corton Ridge, Corton Hill, Windmill Hill, Wheatsheaf Hill – the names on the map are indicative of this beautiful slice of landscape. Cadbury Castle, however, is what the visitors come to see. Its steep, thickly wooded slopes rise to a wide flat plateau nearly a mile around, enclosed by four circles of great grassy ramparts. It is a fine vantage point, which for centuries has looked out across the surrounding countryside. Sometimes what was seen brought anxiety and terror, on other occasions triumph, whilst to today's visitor the most common feeling is one of pure contentment.

Deep in the heart of South Somerset, almost on the Dorset border, lies one of the most exciting antiquities in the whole of Somerset – South Cadbury Castle, to many the site of Arthur's Camelot. It stands as the northern outpost of an area of fine hill country where the slopes drop,

The **Red Lion**, constructed from the mellow stone that is quarried on Ham Hill, very much resembles a double-fronted cottage. Fine real ales are available, as well as home-made tasty snacks, which include jacket potatoes and sandwiches, ploughman's and crusty rolls. For larger appetites, there is a range of meat and fish dishes. The Red Lion's beer garden, lying in the shadow of Cadbury Castle, is quite the perfect place to rest and linger awhile following an energetic walk on the hills of South Somerset.

Opening times are 12 noon to 2.30 pm and 7 pm to 11 pm on Monday to Friday (closed Tuesday lunchtime); 12 noon to 3 pm and 7 pm to 11 pm on Saturday; 12 noon to 3 pm and 7 pm to 10.30 pm on Sunday.

Telephone: 01963 440448.

Distance: 6 miles

OS Explorer 129 Yeovil and Sherborne GR 632256

Tracks, fieldpaths and lanes that cross a hilly landscape in South Somerset

---

Starting point: The free public car park in South Cadbury.

How to get there: South Cadbury lies just south of the A303 trunk road at Chapel Cross, 2 miles east of Sparkford. The public car park is on the village's main street, 200 yards from the Red Lion, past the church. There is also room for careful roadside parking around the inn.

The Walk

1 Leave the car park in South Cadbury, turn left and walk for 400 yards to a road junction. Ignoring the side turn on the left – Crang's Lane – follow the main lane ahead for just 50 yards to a stile on the left. Cross this stile, and drop downhill to the next stile in the opposite field boundary and a footbridge over a stream. Beyond this bridge, cross the field ahead to a track in the far left corner, just to the right of a barn. At the start of this track, turn right by a marker post down to a stile and open field. Turn left and walk across the top left edge of this field to a stile in the corner, before following the top left edge of the next field to its corner. Turn right along the end field boundary, taking the track down to Whitcombe Farm. Follow the lane beyond the farm up to a small green and road junction, turn left and, in 30 yards, turn left and follow a lane that begins to climb steadily up Corton Hill.

2 In 500 yards, at the top of the climb, turn sharp right along a track to a gate and stile and follow the line of the fence ahead. On reaching a corner formed by this fence, turn left and follow the line of the fence across Corton Hill – the detour to the trig point ahead being almost obligatory! –

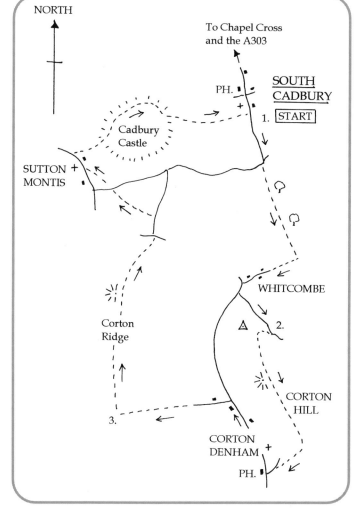

NORTH

To Chapel Cross and the A303

PH.

SOUTH CADBURY

1. START

Cadbury Castle

SUTTON MONTIS

WHITCOMBE

Corton Ridge

2.

CORTON HILL

3.

CORTON DENHAM

PH.

for 300 yards to a gate, then continue alongside the next fence across the hilltop to the corner of the following field. On reaching the far side of the field, make for a gate in the end field boundary, 30 yards down from the corner of the field. Beyond this gate, follow a grassy path downhill towards Corton Denham until, almost in the bottom corner of the field, pass through a gate in the fence on the right to join a back lane. Turn left to follow this lane down to the main road in the village. Turn right and follow this road through the village for 400 yards before turning left into Ridge Lane. Follow this lane for ½ mile until it ends at a pair of gates.

The delightful church in Sutton Montis

❸ Pass through the right-hand gate, turn right and follow the top right edges of three fields across Corton Ridge. Pass through a gate in the end field boundary of the third field, and follow the path ahead as it bears right around Parrock Hill. In 200 yards, bear left down to a gate and follow an enclosed path through a line of trees down to a lane. Follow the road opposite – slightly to the left – towards South Cadbury. In 150 yards, just past a track, cross a stile and head diagonally across the middle of the field ahead to a stile in the far corner and walk ahead to a lane. Pass through the kissing gate opposite, and walk diagonally across an orchard to a gate before following the left edge of a paddock to a gate and the lane in Sutton Montis. Turn right, pass the church and, in 200 yards, immediately past a stream, follow a footpath on the right into a field. Turn right and walk across to a stile above the stream that lies in the dip on the right. Walk across the next field and, where the fence on the left ends, walk uphill – bearing left all the

while – to a stile at the entrance to the woodland surrounding the western slopes of Cadbury Castle. Follow the steep path uphill through the trees to emerge on the open hilltop. Turn left and follow the ramparts around to the north-east corner of the hillfort. Join a track, and follow this track downhill to the road in South Cadbury – turn right back to the car park and left to the Red Lion.

Place of Interest

The **Haynes Motor Museum** is located in Sparkford, just a couple of miles west of South Cadbury. The publicity material says it all: 'Travel through motoring history at Britain's most spectacular international collection of historic cars from around the world. You've loved them, you've loathed them, or you've lusted after them – now they're all under one roof. A hundred years of fascinating motoring history awaits you and your family at the Haynes Motor Museum.' Telephone 01963 440804 for more details.

Date walk completed:

....

The Blue Ball Hotel

The abbey dovecote still stands, but the Augustinian priory is long gone, only a mysterious isolated wall remaining. To the north of the town lies some remarkably hilly countryside that forms the focus of this walk. Hidden sunken tracks climb the hillside to reach Creech Hill Farm, whose hilltop location offers a fine vantage point across to Alfred's Tower and the woodland bordering the Stourhead Estate. This part of Somerset in certainly far from the proverbial madding crowd, the perfect spot to rest awhile and restore that contented mien.

Bruton is a delightful old town, deep in the Somerset hills, whose original wealth came from medieval woollen and silk industries. There is a great sense of religious history in the town, too, dating back to the arrival of Augustinian monks in 1150 who upgraded the local priory to an abbey.

The **Blue Ball** sits proudly at the eastern end of Bruton's High Street, surrounded by attractive stone cottages, houses, shops and other business premises. The stonework is now hidden beneath white plasterwork but, in keeping with its name, blue paintwork adorns the exterior of this fine old hostelry. The delicious menu ranges from starters, light snacks, baguettes and grilled paninis through to main courses that could include sausage and mash, chilli or chicken curry, as well as a number of vegetarian dishes.

Distance: 4 miles

OS Explorer 142 Shepton Mallet and Mendip Hills East
GR 684349

Tracks, fieldpaths and lanes that cross a moderately hilly landscape

Starting point: Silver Street car park (free) in Bruton, 5 minutes walk from the Blue Ball.

How to get there: Follow the A359 around the one-way system in Bruton and, just 50 yards past the church, turn right into the easily missed and unmarked Silver Street car park.

Opening times are 12 noon to 2 pm and 5 pm to 11 pm on Monday and Wednesday to Friday; 5 pm to 11 pm (only) on Tuesday; 12 noon to 3 pm and 6.30 pm to 11 pm on Saturday; 12 noon to 3 pm and 7.30 pm to 10.30 pm on Sunday.

Telephone: 01749 812315.

The Walk

❶ Cross the footbridge over the River Brue at the end of the car park, and follow the footpath ahead uphill to Bruton's High Street. Turn left and, almost at the end of the High Street, turn right opposite Mill Lane into Mill Dam, just before Truffles Restaurant. Follow what becomes an enclosed footpath for 250 yards and, having passed a ford, follow a lane uphill to the right towards some cottages. In 75 yards, turn left along a track signposted 'Huish Lane'. In 200 yards, having crossed a footbridge over a stream, follow an enclosed track on the left that climbs gently uphill out of the valley bottom. In ¾ mile, where the track bears left down to a road, pass through a wooden handgate on the right to follow a bridleway. Cross the field ahead – bearing slightly right – to reach a handgate in the opposite hedgerow before dropping down to a track.

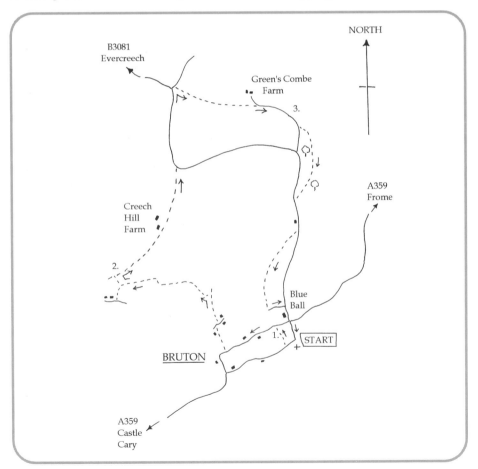

② Turn right and follow an enclosed sunken track uphill for 600 yards until it emerges on the hilltop by Creech Hill Farm. Continue along the drive in front of the farm buildings and go on to its junction with the B3081. Turn left and follow this 'B' road for 500 yards to a junction by a small green. Turn right – signposted to Batcombe – and almost immediately pass through a gateway on the right to join a waymarked bridleway. Follow the line of the hedge on the left around to a gap in the hedgerow in the far left corner of the field, before following a small ridge ahead in the next field. Where this ridge ends, drop down the steep hillside making for a gateway and the drive leading away from Green's Combe Farm some 100 yards to the right of the farm buildings. Join this drive, turn right and, in 200 yards, where the drive begins to bear right, pass through a gateway directly ahead.

③ Head across the field ahead for 200 yards to the end of the line of a hedgerow on the left. At this point, turn right down to a handgate at the bottom of the field. Continue along a path through an area of woodland for 250 yards to an open field, before following the fence ahead along to a gate and the B3081. Turn left and follow the road with care for 250 yards to

Bruton's dovecote stands in splendid isolation

a handgate on the right, just past the driveway leading down to Coombe Farm. Follow the footpath to Bruton ahead across the middle of the field, following the line of the telegraph poles to a handgate on the far side of the field, just above Bruton. Walk down the right edge of the next field for 75 yards to a handgate, and follow an enclosed path downhill to a gate and new estate. Halfway down the estate, turn left along to the Royal Oak Inn and the B3081. Turn right down to the main road in Bruton by the Blue Bell, before following the main road opposite down to the church and the car park.

> **Date walk completed:**
>
> ....

Places of Interest

Bruton's Museum, located in the Dovecote Building in the High Street, depicts the town's rich and varied history. As well as displays relating to the local wool and silk industries from centuries past, the museum offers a new exhibition each year that runs from May through to October. Telephone: 01749 812851. **St Mary's church** in Bruton, with its two towers, is also worth visiting. Internally there is a magnificent roof, but what will first attract is the chancel. This was rebuilt in 1743 and all its original décor is preserved intact. To the south of the church, the **abbey dovecote**, now owned by the National Trust, stands on its hilltop location. Originally built as a tower, it was later converted into a dovecote and is surrounded by two lines of earthworks.

The Salutation

visitor may indeed feel that time has stood still. Ham lies just outside Berkeley, the Gloucestershire town that is best known for its castle and the Edward Jenner Museum. From the village's Salutation pub, the walk follows the Little Avon upstream towards the neighbouring village of Stone, before heading cross-country to the Whitcliff Deer Park. From here there is a fine walk across the hilltop ridge that dominates the park, before returning to Ham and the Salutation. A perfect introduction to the delightful Vale of Berkeley.

Sandwiched between the Cotswold escarpment and the River Severn, the Vale of Berkeley stretches from Frampton-on-Severn in the north down to Thornbury, a commuter town just a few miles north of Bristol. The economy of the Vale is still dominated by small family-owned farms and this lends the area an old-fashioned atmosphere, where the

The **Salutation** is an unpretentious and old-fashioned village local. It almost conveys the impression of being a detached country cottage, with its whitewashed walls, dark paintwork and slate roof, topped with a fine trio of chimney pots. Visitors will enjoy the inn's traditional home-cooked food, with offerings that range from sandwiches and ploughman's through to chicken, fish and steak dishes. A refreshing pint of Flowers or a local cider will provide welcome liquid refreshment at the end of your walk in the Vale of Berkeley, possibly enjoyed in the inn's garden on a fine warm day.

Distance: *6 miles*

OS Outdoor Leisure 14 Wye Valley and Forest of Dean
GR 680983

Fieldpaths and quiet lanes that cross the generally level Vale of Berkeley

Starting point: Salutation Inn at Ham.

How to get there: Follow the A38 to Stone, just north of Thornbury, before taking the B4509 signposted to Ham. The Salutation lies on the right in 2½ miles. Park on the roadside nearby.

Opening times are 11.30 am to 2 pm and 6 pm to 11 pm (closed Monday lunchtime).

Telephone: 01453 810284.

The Walk

1 Walk along the road from the Salutation towards Berkeley. In ¼ mile, the kennels of the local hunt are passed on the right, shortly before you cross the Little Avon. Continue along the road to a footpath on the right signposted to Woodford, just before the Berkeley village sign. Turn right, cross a stream to a gate and enter a field, with a good view of Berkeley Castle. Bear half-right across this field to reach a bridge over the Little Avon some 250 yards distant. Do not cross the river – instead follow the river upstream for 1 mile to Matford Bridge, ignoring an earlier bridge by Brownsmill Farm. Cross the river, turn left along the opposite bank for 50 yards and then turn right past two oak trees, walking away

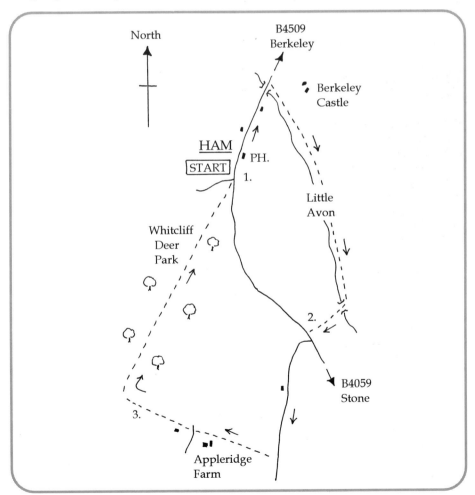

from the Little Avon to reach the corner of the field ahead. Pass through a gateway at this point, and follow the right edges of the next two fields to reach the road running from Ham to Stone.

2 Turn left and, in 100 yards, right along the road signposted to Thornbury and Rockhampton. In ½ mile, just past some cottages on the left, turn right along a potentially very muddy bridleway. In 300 yards, turn right across a footbridge into an adjoining field, before turning left and heading across the field to a stile in the opposite hedgerow by an oak tree. Head across the next field to a stile in the opposite field boundary by a telegraph pole, before making your way across the next field to a stile in the far left-hand corner and a lane. Turn right for a few yards, then left to a gate and stile and hillside field. Head uphill, following the left edge of this field.

3 In the top left corner of this field, cross a stile and turn right to go directly uphill to a gap in the hedgerow above. Follow the path through the trees – with the wall of the deer park on the right – to reach a stepped stile over the wall 150 yards

Berkeley Castle, seen from the walk

before a lodge. Cross into the park, and follow the ridge-top path ahead across the deer park for 1½ miles, with views across the Severn Estuary on the left and the Cotswold Edge on the right. At the far side of the deer park, keep on the path as it drops downhill to a stepped stile at the exit from the park by a farm paddock. Head directly across the field beyond this stile to a gateway and the road from Ham to Stone. Follow the road ahead back into Ham, the Salutation inn appearing shortly on the right.

Date walk completed:

2 0 | 2 | 1 0

Places of Interest

Berkeley lies just a mile to the north of Ham. In 1153, Maurice Berkeley completed work on **Berkeley Castle** at the command of Henry II. Ever since it has been the home of the Berkeley family, who have given their name to many locations all over the world from Berkeley Square in London to Berkeley University in California. Highlights of the castle are the massive Norman keep with the dungeon and the cell where Edward II was murdered in 1327, the picture gallery, the dining room, the medieval buttery and kitchens, the historic great hall and the magnificent apartments. Telephone: 01453 810332.

Also in the town is the **Edward Jenner Museum**, dedicated to the memory of the man and his work. Jenner's study remains much as it was the day he died in 1823. In the peaceful garden is the thatched hut where he vaccinated the poor, free of charge. Telephone: 01453 810631.

The Berkeley Arms

The Severn below Gloucester is not a waterway to be approached lightly. With its huge tidal range, its mud and sand flats and notorious horseshoe bend, only the most seasoned of navigators come this way. To assist access to Gloucester, the Gloucester and Sharpness Canal was cut from Sharpness to the city. Before the walk reaches Sharpness – with its warehouses and cranes, quays and timber yards – our steps cross the fields from neighbouring Purton. The return to Purton is by way of the canal towpath that quite literally runs alongside the Severn Estuary. With views of this great river as well as the remains of the original Severn Bridge – a railway crossing that was destroyed in the 1960s – this is a truly fascinating insight into Gloucestershire's gateway to the sea.

Distance: 4½ miles

OS Outdoor Leisure 14 Wye Valley and Forest of Dean
GR 692042

Level canal towpath and gently undulating fieldpaths

Starting point: The canalside car park in Purton alongside the Gloucester and Sharpness Canal. This is but a few minutes walk from the Berkeley Arms at journey's end.

How to get there: Travelling on the A38, initially aim for Berkeley Road, 15 miles south of Gloucester. From Berkeley Road, follow the unclassified road running west, signposted to Halmore, Purton and Breadstone. In 2 miles, turn right along the lane signposted to Halmore and Purton. In the village, park alongside the canal, opposite the church.

The **Berkeley Arms** is one of a dying breed, a no-frills simple rural pub. It has a tiny bar and one room containing a high backed wooden settle, an upright piano, an open fire in winter and a single window looking out across the river. On warm summer days, the picnic tables outside make a perfect place to rest and linger awhile. Drinks are the focus here, with fine beers such as Wadworth 6X and Fuller's London Pride – as well as a guest ale – always available. For cider lovers, a glass of Stowford Press is highly recommended. The food consists of basic snacks such as rolls and crisps.

Opening times are 7 pm to 11 pm on Monday to Friday (evenings only during the week); 12 noon to 2 pm and 7 pm to 11 pm on Saturday; 12 noon to 2 pm and 7 pm to 10.30 pm on Sunday.

Telephone: 01453 811262.

The Walk

1 Leave the car park and follow the footpath opposite running to the left of St John's church up to a paddock, and cross to a gate in the end field boundary of this small enclosure. In the following field, head uphill – following the line of telegraph poles – to a gate in the top corner of the field and, in the next field, follow the hedge on the right to a gate in the corner. Beyond this gate, head across the following field for 40 yards to a gate on the right, pass into the next field and follow the line of the hedge ahead, with the hedge now on the left. Pass through the handgate in the corner of the field, and follow the field boundary ahead. On reaching the far corner of the field, turn right and walk down the end field boundary for 150 yards to a stile on the

left. Cross into the next field, turn sharp right and walk down to a gate in the right-hand field boundary 50 yards from the corner of the field. Head up the left side of the next field, following a line of telegraph poles. On the far side of the field, 50 yards to the right of a telegraph pole, pass through a gateway and follow the hedge uphill to a gate in the top corner of the field and the lane in the hamlet of Hinton.

2 Turn left along the lane for 75 yards before following a path on the right through a kissing gate into an orchard. Walk down to a gate in the bottom right corner of this orchard and, in the next field, cross to a gate in the left corner. In the following field, make for a gate in its left corner before walking along the right edge of the next field down to a kissing gate in the corner and the road in

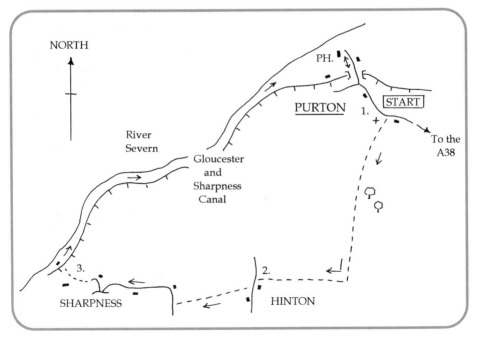

The Gloucester and Sharpness Canal

Sharpness above the docks. Follow the road to the right – it soon bears left in front of a nursing home – and continue over a series of bridges above the docks for 400 yards to a road junction immediately before the sheds and warehouses of Sharpness Docks. Turn right and immediately right again. In 200 yards, just past the access road to the Sharpness Dockers' Club, follow a right turn signposted to Sharpness Marina. Follow this road up to a wooden bungalow called Tintagel then bear left down to a gated car park for the marina.

❸ Follow the path from the car park that slopes downhill to the marina. On reaching the canal, turn left to a bridge, cross the canal and join the towpath. Turn right and follow the towpath for 2 miles back to a swingbridge in Purton and a lane. (**NB:** 250 yards past the abutments of the former railway bridge across the Severn, it is possible to pass through the tree cover on the left and follow the banks of the Severn back towards Purton rather than the canal.) Turn left down to the Berkeley Arms, alongside the River Severn. Having enjoyed sustenance, follow the lane back to the swingbridge, turn left along the canal to the next swingbridge and cross the waterway to return to the car park.

Place of Interest

Slimbridge, with its renowned wildfowl sanctuary, lies just a mile or two north of Purton. Sir Peter Scott's vision became a reality at Slimbridge in 1946, when he realised how many thousands of geese depended on the shores of the Severn Estuary. Today with its award-winning visitor centre overlooking nationally and internationally protected wetlands, this world famous site is an important wintering area for migrating waterbirds such as Bewick's swans and houses the Wildfowl and Wetlands Trust's species conservation programme. Telephone 01453 891992 for further details on opening hours and admission charges.

Date walk completed:

. . . .

treacherous waters, whilst the wooden chest inside the church – carved from a single trunk of elm – was supposedly used for laying out the corpses of those unfortunate enough to have perished in those murky waters. It is below Awre that the world-renowned Severn Bore makes it first appearance when the incoming tides heading up the Severn Estuary are funnelled into a much narrower channel on the approaches to the river's notorious Horseshoe Bend. Alongside the river lie meadows and grazing livestock, whilst the banks are adorned with colours that herald the changing of the seasons. An atmospheric walk, whether it be in the raw air of a winter's morning or accompanied by the passage of the Bore on a balmy summer's evening.

The **Red Hart** was built in the 16th century as lodging for workmen constructing the nearby church, remaining open as a hostelry when the building work was completed. Unusually, there is a glass-covered well in the centre of the main bar. The pub's fine real ales and cuisine are well known in the Forest of Dean. Wherever possible, fresh local ingredients are used in the preparation of dishes, which range from sandwiches and baguettes through to mixed grills and salads. On a warm summer day, the Red Hart's garden is the spot to rest and linger awhile.

Opening times are 12 noon to 3 pm and 6.30 pm to 11 pm on Monday to Friday; 12 noon to 3 pm and 6 pm to 11 pm on Saturday; 12 noon to 3 pm and 7 pm to 10.30 pm on Sunday.

Telephone: 01594 510220.

D ating back to before Saxon times, and with a listing in the Domesday Book, Awre lies alongside the Severn, whose winds and tides have very much moulded the character of the village. Around the churchyard at St Andrew's lie the graves of fishermen who drowned in the river's

Distance: *3½ miles*

OS Outdoor Leisure 14 Wye Valley and Forest of Dean
GR 708080

Level fieldpaths, lanes and flood defences alongside the River Severn

Starting point: The Red Hart at Awre.

How to get there: From Blakeney, on the A48 between Gloucester and Chepstow, follow the unclassified road signposted to Awre. If approaching from Newnham (north of Blakeney), take the turn on the left off the A48 onto an unclassified road to Awre. The Red Hart lies in the centre of the village. There is plentiful roadside parking nearby.

The Walk

1 Leave the pub car park, turn left up to a road junction by the village war memorial and follow the main road ahead. In 300 yards, at a junction by the village hall, follow the cul-de-sac lane on the right – Northington Lane. In 600 yards, where the lane ends at Northington Farm, walk ahead to a gateway to the right of the farmhouse. Continue along an enclosed track to a gateway. Stay on this track as it crosses the left edge of the next field to reach another gateway and

continue down the right edge of the next field to its bottom corner. At this point, bear right down a bank for a few yards before crossing a stile on the right into the adjoining field. Turn left and follow the left edge of this field – passing a pylon – around to a stile on the left in 200 yards. Cross this stile to reach a riverside field.

2 Walk alongside the Severn across two riverside fields. At the far side of the second field, cross a stile into the next field and follow its left edge – below the river defences and out of sight of the river – to a

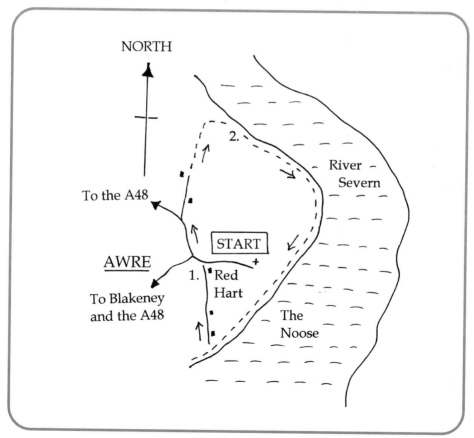

The Severn estuary

stile in the left-hand corner. Turn right for a few yards to the next stile before joining the river defences. Follow the riverbank downstream for ¾ mile to a stile, then walk along the bottom edge of a field to a stile and, in the next field, turn sharp right away from the river to a gate and lane by a farm complex called Whitescourt.

Follow the lane ahead up to the junction by the war memorial in Awre and turn right back to the pub.

Date walk completed:

....

Place of Interest

The **Dean Forest Railway**, a standard gauge heritage railway, operates mainly steam hauled passenger trains between Norchard and Lydney junction, just a few miles down the A48 from Awre. Norchard is the headquarters of the railway, and offers visitors a souvenir shop and museum, a restoration shed and the Coaches Café, which is open on running days. For further information on the railway, including days and hours of operation, telephone 01594 843423.

The Old Crown Inn

hilltops are naturally far-ranging, with landmarks such as the Severn Estuary, the Forest of Dean and the Black Mountains being but the most prominent natural features. As well as the drama of the escarpment, this walk explores the delightful villages of Uley and Nympsfield – where collectively Pevsner found 30 buildings of note – as well as Uley Bury, one of the finest

The most spectacular views and dramatic landscapes within the Cotswolds are to be found in and around the westward-facing escarpment. The hillsides tumble quite precipitously down to the Severn Vale, a drop of over 800 feet in places. The views from the hillforts in the whole of the Cotswold region.

The **Old Crown Inn** is an attractive whitewashed free house, overlooking the green and St Giles' church in Uley. The pub has a lounge and public bar, with exposed beams lending character. Tankards are displayed around the bars, as well as local photographs and prints. A good range of food is available at the Old Crown, extending from sandwiches and jacket potatoes through to grills and daily specials. Uley is home to its own brewery, so no visit to the Old Crown would be complete without a pint of Uley Bitter or Uley Pig's Ear!

Distance: *5 miles*

OS Explorer 168 Stroud, Tetbury and Malmesbury
GR 792986

An energetic walk, with one or two stiff climbs to negotiate

Starting point: The Old Crown Inn in Uley.

How to get there: Uley lies on the B4066 Stroud road, 3 miles east of Dursley. The Old Crown is at the northern end of the village, opposite the church. There is ample room for considerate and careful roadside parking in the vicinity of the inn.

Opening times are 11.30 am to 2.30 pm (3 pm on Saturday) and 7 pm to 11 pm; 12 noon to 3 pm and 7 pm to 10.30 pm on Sunday. Food is normally served from 12 noon to 2 pm and 7 pm to 9 pm.

Telephone: 01453 860502.

The Walk

1 With your back to the Crown, follow the B4066 to the right out of Uley. In 350 yards, turn right into Crawley Lane. Follow this cul-de-sac for 600 yards to a point where it bears right to a detached property. Keep right at this point, and follow the track that climbs uphill into the woodland above this house. In 300 yards, at a junction, keep on the path directly ahead that borders the edge of the woodland. At the next junction in 300 yards – a crossroads – take the right-hand path that again borders the edge of the woodland. Keep on this path as it eventually climbs steeply uphill through Toney Wood to reach a stile and an open grassy area alongside a cottage. Cross this grassy area to a stile and lane.

2 Cross the stile opposite and follow the left edge of a field down to a stile in the corner before continuing down a lane to a road junction in Nympsfield. Turn left up to the Rose and Crown and continue to a junction just past the local school. Turn left and, in 100 yards, follow a footpath

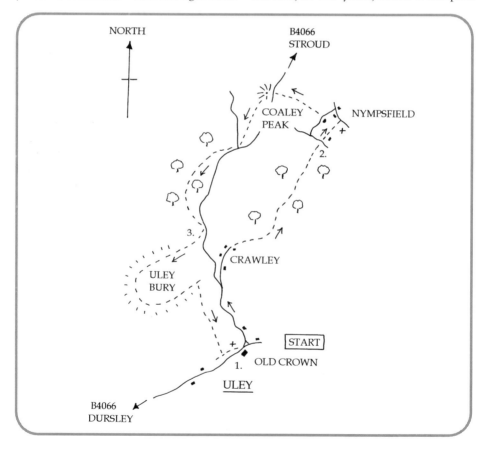

on the right through a gateway. Walk along the right edge of the field ahead to a stile, cross into the next field and follow its left edge to a stile and the B4066. Follow the footpath opposite down into the NT Coaley Peak site. Drop downhill to a junction with another path, turn left and follow what is the Cotswold Way to a gate before continuing for 300 yards through woodland to reach a lane. Turn left, follow this lane up to its junction with the B4066 and take the slip road on the right, which runs parallel to the main road. At the end of this slip road, turn right and follow the signposted Cotswold Way downhill through woodland. At a junction at the bottom of a steep ascent, take the path ahead to the left that begins to climb uphill through the trees. At the next junction, keep left and follow a path beyond a barrier that climbs uphill. Continue for ½ mile to a clearing just beyond a barrier where the Cotswold Way goes off to the right. At this point, turn left up to a gate and the B4066.

❸ Immediately before the main road, follow a bridleway on the right up towards Uley Bury. On reaching the hillfort site, follow the path to the right that follows the north-western edge of the hilltop. In 600 yards, bear left to follow the open south-western edge of the hilltop for 200 yards to the south-eastern corner

Uley's village green

before bearing left to continue along the south-east facing edge. In 600 yards, where the path bears left, follow a footpath on the right that drops down the hillside. Follow the main path down through the woodland for 200 yards to a handgate and open field. Follow the top left edge of this field alongside the woodland, before dropping down the hillside to a handgate in the bottom field boundary a little way to the right of Uley church. Follow the enclosed path beyond this gate down to a junction, turn left and walk along the path that runs besides the church. Keep on this path until it joins the B4066 in Uley by the Old Crown Inn.

Date walk completed:

....

Places of Interest

Hetty Pegler's Tump – or Uley Long Barrow – lies just 1 mile north of Uley alongside the B4066. A Neolithic chambered long barrow some 180 feet in length, it consists of a central passage of stone with three burial chambers.

Owlpen – with its 15th century manor and Victorian church located in a deep wooded hollow – lies just to the east of Uley. Owlpen is worth a visit to enjoy a perfect example of a small Cotswold estate. Telephone: 01453 860261.

Sapperton

The Bell Inn

This short walk explores the Upper Frome Valley high above Stroud, where we find the decaying remains of the Thames and Severn Canal piercing the Cotswold plateau by means of the Sapperton Tunnel. This is an area of steep-sided wooded valleys, quite beautiful in the autumn months when it is clear why the locality is shown as the 'Golden Valley' on local maps. Just occasionally, a view is afforded from some isolated vantage point, and quite dramatic and far-ranging these views turn out to be. Lovers of Cotswold architecture will find a great deal to behold in the small village of Sapperton. St Kenhelm's church, with its Jacobean woodwork and stone monuments, is an absolute gem. The walk also encompasses no fewer than three fine nature reserves – the ancient deciduous tree cover of Siccaridge Wood, the rich wetlands of the Sapperton Valley and the limestone grassland of Daneway Bank. Altogether a quite exceptional walk in a much-loved corner of the 'wolds.

The **Bell Inn**, a 250 year old pub, has been extensively refurbished and enlarged in recent years, the end result being three welcoming bars with flagstone floors, wooden tables and chairs, traditional prints, fresh flowers and wintertime log fires. The excellent meals – that might typically include guinea fowl or lamb shank – use as far as is possible fresh, local ingredients. The local theme extends to the real ales, as well, with brews such as Hook Norton Best and Uley Old Spot usually available for customers. On a warm summer day, there are few more pleasant places to enjoy welcome refreshments than the inn's very pretty courtyard.

Opening times are 11 am to 2.30 pm and 6.30 pm to 11 pm on Monday to Saturday; 12 noon to 3 pm and 7 pm to 10.30 pm on Sunday.

Telephone: 01285 760298.

Distance: *3½ miles*

OS Explorer 168 Stroud, Tetbury and Malmesbury
GR 948033

Steep hillsides and a deep valley, with an easy section of canal towpath

Starting point: The Bell Inn at Sapperton.

How to get there: From the A419 Cirencester to Stroud road, turn off 4 miles west of Cirencester, taking the unclassified road signposted to Sapperton. On approaching the village, follow the signs for the Bell Inn. There is plentiful roadside parking near this hostelry.

The Walk

1 With your back to the Bell, follow the lane to the right for 150 yards to a left-hand bend. At this point, turn right along a cul-de-sac lane that runs past the church. Follow this lane downhill into a valley for 300 yards and, where the lane ends at the entrance to a private property, take the footpath that runs to the left of the property. Follow this path into the valley bottom – deep in Dorvel Wood – cross the infant River Frome and walk uphill along the woodland path ahead for 200 yards to reach a cross track. Follow this track to the left for ¾ mile to a wooden handgate and a lane. Turn left for just a few yards before crossing a stile on the right to join a footpath. Pass through the gateway ahead, and walk the whole length of a hillside field bedecked in limestone grassland to reach a stile in the end field boundary some 400 yards distant.

2 Cross the lane coming up from the Daneway Inn, and follow the path opposite into Siccaridge Wood. Follow the woodland path ahead for ½ mile to reach a staggered crossroads. Take the path ahead - slightly to the left – and at the next junction, bear left and follow a steep woodland path downhill to a bridge over the Thames and Severn Canal. Cross this bridge, turn left and follow the towpath for ¾ mile to the lane by the Daneway, the towpath changing banks at the one footbridge along the way.

3 Turn right, cross the canal bridge and immediately turn left to follow the line of the canal below the pub – the car park is

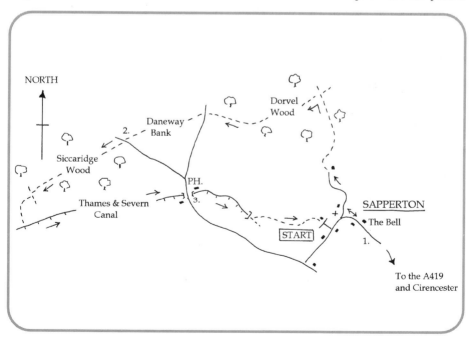

NORTH

Dorvel Wood

Daneway Bank

2.

Siccaridge Wood

PH.

Thames & Severn Canal

3.

START

SAPPERTON

The Bell

1.

To the A419 and Cirencester

On the towpath of the Thames and Severn Canal

built over the canal bed – before rejoining the towpath and continuing for 400 yards to the western portal of Sapperton Tunnel. Follow the footpath above the portal to a stile and enter a hillside field. Bear half-right uphill to the top edge of this field, and follow the top field boundary to the left as far as a handgate. Beyond this gate, follow a footpath up to a back lane by a property. Cross this lane and continue uphill to the main road in Sapperton. Follow this road to the left back around to the Bell Inn.

Date walk completed:

....

Places of Interest

Nearby **Cirencester**, often referred to as the 'capital of the Cotswolds', is an historic Roman town located quite appropriately on the Foss Way. The various Roman relics that have been discovered in the area – including a number of mosaics, a section of Roman wall and a magnificent amphitheatre – are well documented in the town's **Corinium Museum**. In the market square **St John's church** is one of the finest town churches in England, rivalling many cathedrals. The tower was begun early in the 15th century, and the great South Porch was built in 1490. For further information on Cirencester contact the Tourist Information Centre on 01285 654180.

The New Inn

Coln St Aldwyns was once described as one of the ten most desirable villages in England by *Country Life* magazine. With its delightful cottages, its ancient church and its pastoral meadows set alongside the River Coln, it is not difficult to see why this settlement was rated so highly. Above Coln St Aldwyns lies the Saltway, taking our steps across country to the neighbouring village of Bibury. This ancient path was used in the conveyance of salt from Droitwich Spa through to markets across the Cotswolds and deep into South Gloucestershire. Bibury itself – with neighbouring Arlington – is a tourist honeypot. From the 19th century Swan Hotel to the Bibury Trout Farm, from Arlington Mill to St Mary's church, there are attractions at every turn. Perhaps best known is Arlington Row, originally a rank of cottages occupied by weavers who used the small millstream in front of their homes to wash and dye cloth before it was 'racked' to dry on nearby Rack Isle. The River Coln between Bibury and Coln provides the perfect antidote to the crowds who throng the villages in this corner of the 'wolds.

The **New Inn** at Coln – a misnomer if ever there were one! – dates from the 16th century. Back then it was known as 'Ye Olde Inne'. Today it is one of the most highly rated inns in Britain, serving fine real ales, quality wines, exceptional bar food and wonderful restaurant meals.

Opening times are 12 noon to 3 pm and 6 pm to 11 pm on Monday to Saturday; 12 noon to 3 pm and 7 pm to 10.30 pm on Sunday.

Telephone: 01285 750651.

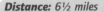

Distance: *6½ miles*

OS Outdoor Leisure 45 The Cotswolds GR 146050

Tracks, fieldpaths and lanes that cross a gently undulating landscape

Starting point: The New Inn at Coln St Aldwyns.

How to get there: From the A417, turn off 5 miles east of Cirencester by an isolated pub to the east of Ampney St Peter, following the unclassified road signposted to Coln St Aldwyn. In 5 miles, this road reaches the New Inn on the right. There is room for careful roadside parking around the inn.

The Walk

1 Walk up the main street from the New Inn to a junction in the middle of Coln St Aldwyns, alongside the post office. Follow the road opposite signposted to Bibury and, in 150 yards, cross a stile on the left just past the last property on the left. Walk diagonally across the field ahead to a stile in the opposite field boundary – almost in the left corner – and join a lane. Follow this lane to the left for ¾ mile before forking right along a waymarked public path. Follow this track for 350 yards and, where the line of trees on the left ends, keep ahead along the grassy path that heads across the middle of the

field to a handgate on the far side. Beyond this gate, continue along the grassy path as it crosses the left edge of the field to a gap in the opposite field boundary, before heading across the middle of the following field to a gap in an old stone wall. Head across one final field, passing a telegraph pole along the way, then reach a gate and the B4425.

2 Cross the main road, and follow a well-defined track opposite for 600 yards across two fields. On reaching a junction, pass through a gateway on the left and walk down the right edge of the field ahead to a gate at the far end and Hale Barn. Follow the track to the left of the

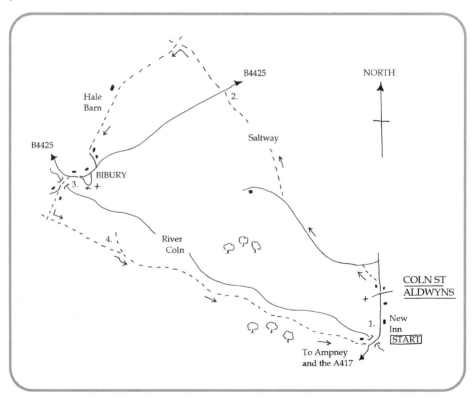

barn and, in 250 yards, where a track bears left across to Bibury Farm, keep on the track ahead that heads in a southerly direction to reach a reservoir on the left. Beyond the reservoir, follow the right of way along the left edges of two fields before reaching a property on the left. Follow the drive beyond this property as it winds its way down to the B4425 in Bibury. Turn right and, in a few yards, pass through a gap in the wall on the left by a telephone box. Follow a back lane down into the village, keeping right at the entrance to the church to continue back to the B4425.

The famous Arlington Row

③ Follow the main road ahead alongside the Coln, before turning left to cross the river at the first footbridge. Stay on the path past Arlington Row, and continue up the lane ahead – Hawkers Hill – to a junction on the hilltop. Follow the gravel road ahead up between properties to a handgate, before continuing along a short section of enclosed path to another handgate and an open field. Follow the right edge of the field ahead and, just inside the next field, turn left and follow the field boundary on the left to the corner of the field. Join an enclosed footpath, and continue ahead for 250 yards to a gate and stile. Keep on the path as it runs along the left edge of a field alongside a belt of trees to a handgate, before continuing along an enclosed track for 200 yards down to a junction.

④ Turn right and continue along the track for 650 yards until it drops downhill to reach a stile and meadow bordering the

Coln. Bear half-left across this meadow to a gate opposite, before continuing along an enclosed path through some woodland to the next gate and meadow. Cross the meadow, with the river away to the left, to reach a gate on the far side of the field. Continue along the riverside path as it crosses two fields and, just as the path enters a third field, fork right to follow a waymarked path away from the Coln towards an area of woodland. Follow the path alongside – and eventually through – the woodland to reach a gate at the far end of the tree cover and a meadow. Cross to a gate on the far side of the field, pass alongside Yew Tree Lodge and join a road. Turn left and follow this road back to the New Inn in Coln St Aldwyns.

Place of Interest

For details of nearby **Cirencester**, see Walk 32.

Date walk completed:

....

107

The Seven Tuns

Chedworth Roman Villa, with its fine mosaics and bathhouses, hypocausts and water shrine, as well as a recently constructed museum that provides visitors with a fascinating insight into the way of life in this remote valley all those years ago. Deep in Chedworth Woods, just above the villa, lie the remains of the long disused railway that ran from Cheltenham through the Cotswolds towards the South Coast. A mile of the former trackbed now forms the Chedworth Nature Reserve, where exposed Cotswold limestone, lime-rich springs and ancient beech woodland provide habitats for a rich array of flora and fauna that includes bats and deer, dormice, lizards and even Roman snails whose ancestors were imported by the ancient Romans!

Chedworth is an attractive Cotswold village, whose traditional stone cottages and houses hug the steep sides of a tributary valley of the Coln. In the neighbouring valley lies

Distance: *4½ miles*

*OS Outdoor Leisure 45 The Cotswolds
GR 053120*

Steep hillsides, valleys and shady woodland in the heart of the Cotswolds

Starting point: The public car park beside Chedworth church, immediately above the Seven Tuns.

How to get there: From the A429 between Cirencester and Northleach, turn off westwards 7 miles from Cirencester, signposted to Chedworth village – not the Roman villa – just ½ mile north of Foss Cross and the Hare and Hounds. Follow this unclassified road for 2 miles to a sharp right turn signposted to Chedworth and Yanworth. As you enter Chedworth, turn left along a cul-de-sac lane just above the Seven Tuns and park by the church.

This attractive 17th century **Seven Tuns** inn, with its traditional bars, is wonderfully atmospheric, whilst nothing could be more tranquil than sitting outside the pub on a warm summer's day watching water cascading from one of the local springs. A range of Young's beers is available at the Seven Tuns, including their Bitter, Special and seasonal ales, as well as a regular guest beer. There is also an excellent range of home-made food.

Opening times are 12 noon to 3 pm and 6 pm to 11 pm on Monday to Saturday; 12 noon to 3 pm and 7 pm to 10.30 pm on Sunday (no food on a Sunday evening).

Telephone: 01285 720242.

The Walk

1 Take the grassy path in front of some cottages down to the Seven Tuns, turn left and follow the lane through Chedworth. Head out of the village by way of a steep hill and, having reached the hilltop, follow the road across open country for ½ mile to a point where a footpath crosses the road. Pass through the gate on the left, and head directly across the field ahead to a prominent sycamore tree. Beyond this tree, follow the path that drops downhill – bearing slightly right – to the entrance to Chedworth Woods. Follow the main path ahead for 600 yards, before forking left along a waymarked grassy path up to another track. Turn right and, in a short distance, keep left at a fork to continue along the waymarked path for 150 yards

to a stile at the exit from the woodland.

2 Turn left and, where the lane bears right to cross the infant River Coln, keep ahead along a private road – a public footpath. Follow this track for just over 1 mile to a road junction just below Chedworth Roman Villa. Turn left and follow the lane up to the entrance to the villa. Follow the path that passes to the left of the National Trust complex into Chedworth Woods. In 100 yards, pass under an old railway line – a detour to the left brings you to the former trackbed, now the Chedworth Nature Reserve – and continue uphill for 200 yards to a crossroads.

3 Turn left and follow the woodland path for 400 yards to the exit from the

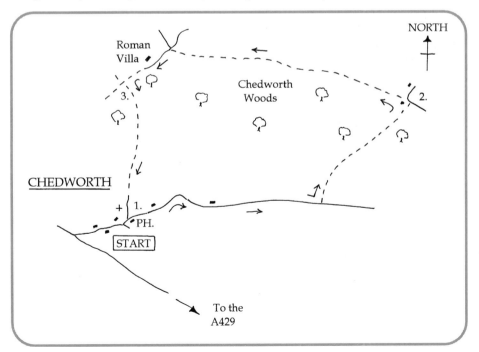

Chedworth

woodland. Head uphill across the field ahead to a fence, before following the line of this fence – with the fence on the left – to a gate in the corner of the field. Follow a short section of enclosed path ahead, before following some steps downhill into a long open field. Walk across this field and, on approaching the far side of the

field, bear right to a stile and lane by a property. Follow this lane along to Chedworth church.

Date walk completed:

....

Places of Interest

Northleach, just a few miles north of Chedworth, is a delightful Cotswold town, with a market place bordered by half-timbered buildings and merchants' houses dating from the 16th century. At the crossroads at the entrance to the town stands the great 'House of Correction', dating from the era of severe sharp punishments! Reminders of the great days of the wool trade are everywhere in the town, most evidently the impressive church of St Peter and St Paul, a fine example of the Cotswold Perpendicular style.

One of the most fascinating attractions in Northleach is Keith Harding's **World of Mechanical Music**. This museum occupies the Oak House, once home to a wealthy wool merchant, and contains a collection of instruments in the old school room, including barrel pianos, musical boxes, polyphons and automata. For more information, visit www.mechanicalmusic.co.uk

The Falcon Inn

17th and 18th centuries. It was the dyed cloth trade that predominated in this area, with the local streams and springs offering some of the purest water to be found in the West Country. Across the valley from Painswick lies Slad, forever immortalised in Laurie Lee's *Cider with Rosie*. The landscape hereabouts is stunning, with deep valley bottoms, steep hillsides, ancient woodlands and quite exceptional views across a truly atmospheric and evocative corner of Gloucestershire.

Painswick, located on a spur high above two archetypal Cotswold villages, owes its wealth and reputation to the woollen industry that dominated the local economy back in the

Distance: *5 miles*

OS Explorer 179 Gloucester, Cheltenham and Stroud
GR 865095

Steep hillsides, plunging valleys and shady woodland in the heart of the Cotswolds

Starting point: The public car park alongside the A46 at the southern end of Painswick, just a few minutes walk from the Falcon Inn, which is passed at the end of the walk.

How to get there: Painswick lies on the main A46 Cheltenham road, 3 miles north of Stroud. There is a well signposted public car park at the southern end of the town (fee payable).

The Falcon Inn is located on the charming high street of the small Cotswold town of Painswick, known as the Queen of the Cotswolds. The inn has a fascinating history. Built in 1554, it served as a courthouse as well as a licensed house from the 17th century. Until the advent of the motoring age, the Falcon was the principal coaching inn and posting house for the region. Today, with its Cotswold stone exterior and warm traditional bars, it has an atmosphere that really is that little bit special. Traditional warmth abounds, with stone floors, wintertime log fires and a menu that changes each week, offering an excellent cuisine.

Opening times are rather more flexible than a traditional hostelry, as the Falcon is also a hotel. Meals are normally served each day from 12 noon to 2 pm and 7 pm to 9 pm.

Telephone: 01452 814222.

The Walk

1 Leave the car park at its southern end, and turn left along Stamages Lane away from the A46. Drop downhill into the valley bottom and, in 400 yards, cross a stream before beginning to climb uphill. In 40 yards, just past a property called Byeways, turn right along a lane signposted to Sheephouse. Continue on this access lane for 600 yards and, immediately before the property called Sheephouse, turn left and pass through a small squeeze-belly stile. Follow an enclosed footpath around the edge of Sheephouse and its grounds and on uphill to another squeeze-belly stile. Walk uphill along the left edge of the field ahead to a stile on the left, cross the stile and follow the right edge of the next field uphill to a stile in the top corner of the field and a lane. Turn left and, at a junction in 40 yards, take the right turn to Bulls Cross and Birdlip.

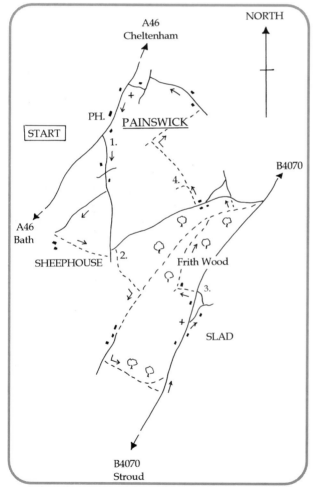

2 Almost immediately, turn right along a stony track and continue uphill – ignoring all side turns – for 600 yards to reach an open hilltop field. Cross to the far side of this field, before turning right along a side track and walking along to Worgan's Farm. Pass the farm buildings and, 50 yards past the last property on the right, cross a stile on the left and follow an enclosed footpath downhill through Worgan's Wood to a stile and open field. Follow the left edge of this field down to a gate, and continue along a track for 150 yards to a sharp left turn. At this point, pass through the handgate ahead and follow a footpath down to the B4070. Cross to the pavement opposite and follow the road to the left into Slad. Continue for 250 yards past the Woolpack Inn and the church, and where the pavement ends, fork right along a back lane called Steanbridge Lane, which runs parallel to the main road. In 200 yards, where the main lane bears sharply right, follow the lane ahead that climbs uphill to the left to reach a war memorial by the B4070.

❸ Cross the main road and follow the lane opposite up to a property on the right. Immediately past this property, turn right along a bridleway leading into Frith Wood Nature Reserve. Follow the main track again, climbing steadily all the while and ignoring all side turns, for 600 yards to a junction in a clearing on the hilltop. Turn right and follow a track through the woodland for 350 yards to a gate. Just past this gate, turn left down a track to reach a lane and junction in 100 yards. Turn left and follow a lane for 150 yards to a junction by a property called Red Stables. Follow the lane ahead for 100 yards and, immediately past the drive on the right leading to Painswick Heights, turn right along an unmetalled track.

❹ In 120 yards, where this track bears left, cross a stile and enter a hillside field with a fine view across to Painswick. Follow the left edges of two fields and, in the corner of the second field, cross a stile and follow an enclosed path downhill into the valley. In 300 yards, keep on this path as it bears right to run just above the valley bottom. Follow this path – it becomes a tarmac drive – for 600 yards to a lane below Painswick, ignoring one early left fork down to a property. Turn left, pass Brookhouse Mill, and follow the lane ahead steeply uphill for 300 yards to

Painswick

a junction in Painswick, just past Golden Hart House. Turn left towards Painswick church, before bearing right up to the A46. On reaching the main road, turn left and follow the A46 down past the church and the Falcon Inn to return to the car park on the left.

Places of Interest

Stroud - just south of Painswick - was built on steep hillsides at the junction of no fewer than five valleys that converge on the town. This was arguably the major cloth centre in the Cotswolds for more than five centuries with, at its peak, over 150 mills being located in the surrounding valleys. Of particular interest is Stroud's new family-friendly **museum** set in attractive parkland. The innovative and colourful displays include dinosaurs and mammoth remains, Roman altars, landscape paintings and two of the earliest lawnmowers! Visitors can also find out about local history, as well as family and working life in the Cotswold Hills and Severn Valley in years gone by. Telephone the museum on 01453 763394 for more details.

Date walk completed:

....

The Glasshouse Inn

May Hill is, I suspect, Gloucestershire's best known yet least visited landmark. Its 971 foot summit, decked out with a clump of pine trees, is familiar to the millions of motorists who travel up and down the M5 motorway between Bristol and Worcester each year. Equally, many walkers following the Cotswold Way will have pointed out the round mass of old red sandstone with its crown of trees that marks the real boundary of the English plain. Beyond rise the foothills of the Welsh mountains. Few travellers, however, venture towards the Herefordshire border to seek out this lonely and isolated spot. The effort is well worthwhile for, in addition to the quite magnificent views over many neighbouring counties, the walk brings the opportunity to stroll through the Newent Woods. As a seasonal excursion, springtime is especially rewarding as the woodland bursts into colour with wild daffodils and bluebells.

The **Glasshouse Inn** is named after migrant glass workers from Lorraine who, in order to meet the growing demand for glass in England during the 17th century, established a works in this corner of Gloucestershire where timber for fuel was abundant. An unspoiled, family-run, award-winning pub with original quarry tiled flooring, the Glasshouse serves real ale straight from the cask, whilst the excellent pub food is available every day of the week except Sundays. On hot summer's days, the peaceful garden with its cider press and canopies formed by yew trees is the ideal place to enjoy liquid refreshment.

Distance: 4½ miles

OS Outdoor Leisure 14 Wye Valley and Forest of Dean
GR 709214

A gentle woodland stroll through to Clifford's Mesne, before a challenging climb onto May Hill itself

Starting point: The small green opposite the Glasshouse Inn at Glasshouse.

How to get there: Glasshouse lies one mile north of Dursley Cross, midway between Gloucester and Ross-on-Wye on the A40. Follow the signposts to Glasshouse, and park on the green opposite the Glasshouse Inn.

Opening times are 11.30 am to 3 pm and 6 pm to 11 pm on Monday to Saturday; 12 noon to 2.30 pm and 7 pm to 10.30 pm on Sunday.

Telephone: 01452 830529.

The Walk

1 From the parking area, follow the road opposite the Glasshouse Inn signposted to Clifford's Mesne. In 200 yards, follow a signposted footpath on the right that crosses the corner of a field to reach a stile at the entrance to Newent Woods. In just 30 yards, at a junction,

follow the footpath opposite that heads off into the heart of the woodland. At the next junction in 350 yards, turn left and follow a path for another 350 yards to a junction with a prominent forest track. Cross this track, and continue along the faint path opposite through the bracken for 80 yards to reach another forestry track. Walk ahead along this track,

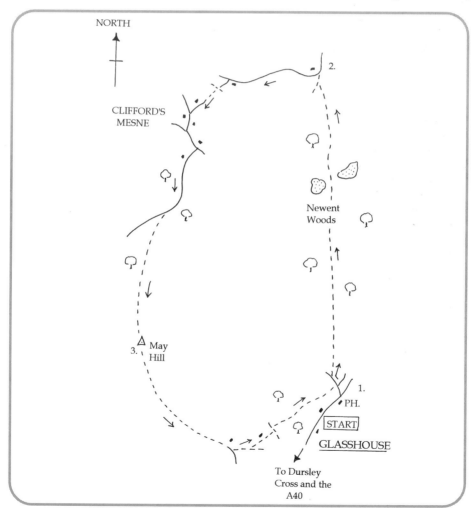

NORTH

CLIFFORD'S
MESNE

2.

Newent
Woods

3. △ May
Hill

1.

● PH.

START

GLASSHOUSE

To Dursley
Cross and the
A40

passing Huntley Pond, before continuing along a narrower path to reach a junction of tracks. Take the main track across an open clearing to reach a gate and a junction with another track. Follow this track ahead down to a lane.

Friendly ponies on May Hill

2 Follow this lane to the left towards Clifford's Mesne and, in 600 yards, at a junction just past a property on the left, fork left along a side lane. Follow this lane for 150 yards to a crossroads, and continue ahead along a grassy byway. Keep on this byway – it becomes a tarmac road running past houses – to the next junction, turn left and continue along the road in Clifford's Mesne to the next junction by a small green. Keep left at this junction towards Glasshouse and, in 100 yards, turn right along the lane that heads up to the Yew Tree Restaurant. Follow this lane uphill for 500 yards to a cattle grid, before turning left to follow a path signposted to May Hill that climbs up through the bracken covered hillside. In 600 yards, pass through a handgate and walk across the open hilltop ahead to reach the clump of trees atop May Hill.

3 Walk through the clump of trees to the trig point, and continue down the hillside ahead to a handgate and National Trust

sign in 250 yards. Keep on downhill along an enclosed path and, at a junction in 300 yards, fork left into woodland. In just 80 yards, fork left at a junction and follow the path ahead to a junction in 250 yards, just past a property on the left. Turn left at this junction, and walk along to a handgate at the entrance to the Huntley Estate. Just past this gate, turn right along a path waymarked as the Wysis Way, and continue along a path through Newent Woods for just over ½ mile to a gate and lane. Turn right back to the green in Glasshouse.

Date walk completed:

....

Places of Interest

The **National Birds of Prey Centre** at Newent lies just a mile or two north of Glasshouse. It houses one of the oldest and certainly the best known and respected specialist collection of birds of prey in the world – approximately 250 birds of over 85 species. Telephone: 0870 990 1992; website: www.nbpc.co.uk

The **Three Choirs Vineyard** near Newent is now one of Gloucestershire's main attractions, offering a unique experience both for wine enthusiasts and those just looking for a relaxing and beautiful environment in which to enjoy an outing. Visitors can enjoy occasional wine tasting sessions. Telephone: 01531 890223; website: www.three-choirs-vineyards.co.uk

The Haw Bridge Inn

H aw Bridge is the first crossing point on the River Severn upstream of Gloucester. The Severn Navigation extends upstream as far as Stourport, although the only commercial traffic on the river today consists of the commercial barges carrying grain to the Allied Mills in Tewkesbury. In centuries past, barges carried coal up the river from the Forest of Dean, and the Coombe Hill Canal was constructed from the river to give easier access to Cheltenham. The canal closed in 1876 but, together with 178 acres of surrounding wet meadowland, it now forms the Coombe Hill Canal Nature Reserve. These watery elements form the focus of this walk deep in the heart of North Gloucestershire.

The attractive **Haw Bridge Inn** enjoys an enviable location fronting onto the River Severn. There is even a floating pontoon so that bargees can moor alongside the inn before enjoying the fine beers available. The bar area is wood panelled, with many artefacts hanging from its ceiling. The area suffers from flooding – and consequent isolation – facts that are well documented in the photographs and pictures that are displayed around the bar area. Being a Wadworth house, their 6X flagship brew should be your natural accompaniment to whichever of the tasty dishes you choose from the menu.

Opening times are 11 am to 3 pm and 6 pm to 11 pm.

Telephone: 01452 780316.

Distance: 5 miles

OS Explorer 179 Gloucester, Cheltenham and Stroud
GR 844278

Quiet lanes, tracks and fieldpaths, with just one gentle climb from the river into Apperley

Starting point: The Haw Bridge Inn at Tirley.

How to get there: Approaching on the A38, turn off 4 miles south of Tewkesbury and follow the B4213 Ledbury road for 4 miles to Haw Bridge and the River Severn. Having crossed the river, turn immediately left to park on the lane by the inn.

The Walk

❶ Return to the B4213, cross to the pavement opposite and go over the River Severn. On the far side of Haw Bridge, turn left through a gateway and follow the Severn Way across two fields to a stile at the entrance to a small caravan park. Walk along the footpath through this park to a handgate and a lane by the Coal House Inn. Follow the lane to the right and around to the left behind the Coal House Inn and, just beyond the left-hand bend behind the inn, turn right to follow a signposted path beyond a cattle grid. Ahead is a drive leading to a property – veer right off of this track to reach a gate and stile in the end field boundary. Cross the next field, walking up through a shallow valley, to a stile in the far left corner of the field. Continue ahead uphill in the following field to the top boundary

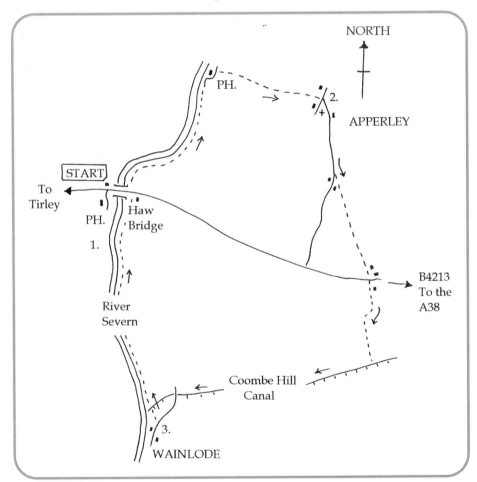

and, beyond the stile, follow the right edge of the field ahead to a gate in the corner before continuing down a track to the lane in Apperley by a green.

2 Two roads go off on the right – take the second right, signposted to Tirley and Gloucester. In 350 yards, immediately before a new housing development called Moore's Ground, turn left along a track and continue for ¼ mile down to the B4213. Cross the road and follow the bridleway opposite for 400 yards to a junction with a track, immediately beyond a footbridge over a ditch. Turn right and follow this track for almost 1 mile to reach a lane, with the Coombe Hill Canal behind the bushes on the left. On reaching the lane, turn left and, in 300 yards, cross a stile on the right just before the Severn to join the Severn Way.

3 Cross the field ahead towards a pylon, pass through a gateway – immediately before which the path goes over the Coombe Hill Canal – and bear left down towards the Severn. Follow the slightly raised flood defence alongside the Severn upstream for ¾ mile, passing through gateways along the way. In ¾ mile, cross a stile and follow the left edge of the field ahead, with the Severn now one field away on the left. Cross a stile in the left corner of this field, walk halfway across the next field before bearing left to a stile and a riverside meadow. Bear right to a stile, and follow a grassy flood defence alongside a property and up to a gate and the B4213. Cross Haw Bridge, and return to the Haw Bridge Inn.

Apperley's church seen from across the pond

Place of Interest
Tewkesbury, just a few miles north of Tirley, lies at the confluence of the Warwickshire Avon and the River Severn. With both these waterways being navigable, the town soon established itself as an inland port. The great Benedictine abbey, almost certain to have replaced a much older church, was founded in the 12th century, but dates mainly from the 11th century. The enormous cylindrical pillars in the nave are the loftiest pillars in the country, and the spectacular central tower, which stands 132 feet high and 46 feet square, making it the largest surviving Norman central tower in the world, continues as a prominent landmark in the town. The west front with its impressive Norman arch of six orders, originally of seven, is one of the finest in England. Tewkesbury's Tourist Information Centre can be contacted on 01684 295027.

Date walk completed:

....

This walk is deliberately low on miles to enable you not only to enjoy the first-class Craven Arms, but also because of the magnificent man-made and natural landscape that will delay your steps. The two villages on the route – Sevenhampton and Brockhampton – are not names that most visitors to the Cotswolds will be familiar with. Lying along unclassified lanes, far from the nearest main road, both take some finding and are all the better for that. Their stone cottages, the inn and St Andrew's church at Sevenhampton lie scattered along the upper reaches of the Coln Valley, hereabouts little more than a small stream. As well as an exploration of these settlements, the walk takes us high onto the 'wolds above the valley. Here, at over 800 feet above sea level, we follow an ancient bridleway that brings with it extensive views across a particularly evocative part of the Cotswolds.

The **Craven Arms** at Brockhampton is a wonderfully traditional hostelry. There are low beams and rough stone walls, pine furniture and wall settles, tiled flooring and a wintertime log fire, This fine 17th century inn also boasts a pleasant garden, an ideal place to rest and linger awhile following a stroll in a fine corner of the Cotswolds. The menu offers some imaginative options – such as goat's cheese and bacon salad or confit of duck leg with redcurrant and port sauce – prepared wherever possible using local ingredients. The Craven Arms also offers customers fine real ales, which might include Hook Norton Best or Fuller's London Pride.

Opening times are 11 am to 3 pm and 6 pm to 11 pm on Monday to Saturday; 12 noon to 4 pm and 7 pm to 10.30 pm on Sunday.

Telephone: 01242 820410.

Distance: *3 miles*

OS Outdoor Leisure 45 The Cotswolds GR 035223

Quiet lanes, tracks and fieldpaths in and around a Cotswold valley

Starting point: The Craven Arms in Brockhampton.

How to get there: Brockhampton lies on an unclassified road that runs across the Cotswolds from the A40 at Andoversford to Winchcombe. The signposted Craven Arms lies almost at the end of a cul-de-sac lane that is signposted from the centre of the village.

The Walk

1 Leave the pub car park and turn right back to the main road in Brockhampton. Turn right and, at a junction by a green, turn left along the lane marked to the Memorial Hall. Follow this lane – it soon bears right – for ¾ mile to a junction on the hilltop. Turn right and follow a hilltop road – signposted Andoversford and Stow – through Baker's Wood and on for ½ mile to a road junction. On reaching the road junction, follow the public path opposite – it is a track – across the hilltop above the Coln Valley. Follow this track for ½ mile to a barn on the right, before continuing for ¼ mile to a point where a bridleway crosses the track.

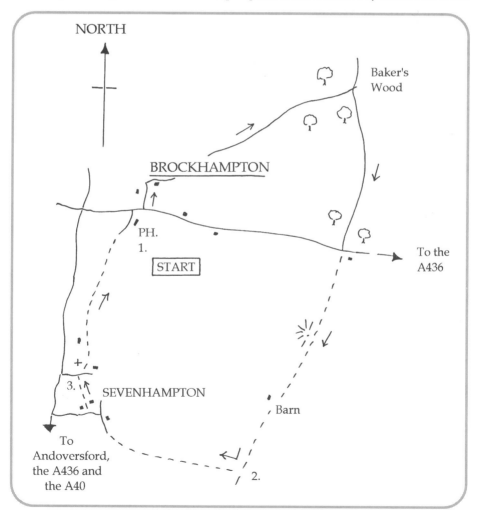

2 Turn right and follow the left edge of a hillside field to a gate in the bottom corner, before following the right edges of the next two fields to reach a gate and a track. Follow this track – it soon bears right – to a gate, and continue along the lane ahead in Sevenhampton to a road junction. Turn left and, immediately before a ford through the Coln, follow a path on the right towards Brockhampton, initially bordering a stream on the left. Follow this path to a footbridge and stile between two properties, before following a grassy path up out of the valley bottom to a kissing gate and field. Cross this field to a gate and the lane by Sevenhampton church.

The Coln valley

3 Enter the churchyard, and follow the path to the right of the church down to a lower burial ground. Walk across the top of this burial ground to a gate in its corner, cross a small enclosure to the next handgate and follow the left edge of the field to a gate in the far corner below Manor Farm. Head straight across the next – much bigger – field to a handgate on the right in the far right corner by a stream. Beyond this gate, follow a path up through some scrubland to join a back lane in Brockhampton that leads to the Craven Arms.

Date walk completed:

....

Places of Interest

Winchcombe is a delightful Cotswold town, just 4 miles north of Brockhampton. The history of this fine settlement from Neolithic times to the present day is told in the local **museum**, which also contains a collection of British and international police uniforms and equipment! Telephone: 01242 609151.

Just to the south-east of Winchcombe is **Sudeley Castle**, one of England's most delightful historic houses, set against the picturesque splendour of rolling Cotswold hills. Telephone: 01242 602308.

Hailes Abbey, another attraction near Winchcombe, enjoys a beautiful setting on the western fringe of the Cotswolds, surrounded by wooded pasture. In the Middle Ages the Cistercian abbey was one of the main centres of pilgrimages in Britain due to a phial possessed by the monks said to contain the blood of Christ. The museum displays include some fine examples of medieval sculpture and decorated floor tiles. Telephone: 01242 602398.

The Old Manse Hotel

crosses undulating countryside to reach Lower and Upper Slaughter. In Lower Slaughter, the cottages sit overlooking Slaughter Brook, whose waters power a brick-built corn mill, now a popular tourist attraction. A few fields away lies Upper Slaughter, with a Norman church, Elizabethan manor and picture postcard cottages centred upon a small green. Bridlepaths and lanes climb the hillsides to the south of the Slaughters to return to the Windrush Valley, with the river being followed back into Bourton-on-the-Water.

No walking tour of the Cotswolds would be complete without a visit to Bourton-on-the-Water – known locally as the 'Venice of the Cotswolds' – and the Slaughters. Even on high days and holidays, when the village is particularly busy, Bourton's crowds are soon left behind as the walk

Recently refurbished, the **Old Manse** was built in 1748 and is a comfortable welcoming hotel, with bar facilities open to non-residents. The name originates from its original function, this fine Cotswold building having been constructed for the local Baptist pastor in 1748. The River Windrush flows just a few feet from the front porch of the hotel, which is a firm favourite with ramblers and tourists alike. A traditional, lively bar serves real ale and excellent bar food – including over 50 sandwich combinations, whilst the delightful, elegant restaurant offers a table d'hôte menu. In the warmth of summer, many visitors enjoy sitting on the fine patio alongside the river, simply watching the world pass by.

Distance: *5 miles*

OS Outdoor Leisure 45 The Cotswolds GR 168205

Once the busy outskirts of Bourton-on-the-Water are left behind, the walk follows fieldpaths, tracks and lanes across the undulating Cotswold landscape

Starting point: The central car park in Bourton-on-the-Water, which lies just a few minutes walk from the Old Manse Hotel in the centre of the village.

How to get there: Leave the A429 Cirencester to Stow road 4 miles south of Stow, and follow the signposted route to Bourton-on-the-Water's main car park (fee payable).

Opening times are rather more flexible than most inns, as the Old Manse is a hotel, but bar meals are available at the normal times of 12 noon to 2 pm and 7 pm to 9.30 pm each day.

Telephone: 01451 820082;
website: www.oldmansehotel.com

The Walk

1 Leave the car park by the main entrance, turn left and follow Station Road for ½ mile around to the main A429. Cross the road using the light-controlled crossing point, turn right and follow the pavement opposite to the right for 100 yards. Just before the Coach and Horses Inn on the right, turn left to follow a signposted footpath across two fields – it has a well-defined tarmac surface – before keeping on the path as it bears right beyond a handgate to head down to the lane in Lower Slaughter. Turn left and, at a fork in 75 yards, keep left and follow the signposted path alongside the River Eye to reach the local mill. Immediately past the mill complex, turn left and follow a footpath that initially runs past the mill and alongside the millstream. In 300 yards, beyond a handgate, walk across

to a gate in the opposite field boundary, bearing slightly right all the while. Walk the whole length of the next field to a handgate in the end field boundary, before following a well-worn path in one final field down to a handgate and footbridge and an enclosed path leading into Upper Slaughter.

2 On reaching the lane in the village, turn right and, in 200 yards, having crossed a stream, turn left along a back lane bearing a 'ford' sign. Walk along to the ford, cross the water by means of a footbridge and follow a lane uphill, passing Upper Slaughter church, to reach a junction. Turn right and continue along the lane past some cottages to a road junction – the left turn is to Bourton, the right turn to Cheltenham. Beyond the gate opposite, follow the footpath ahead – initially it is an enclosed path before it

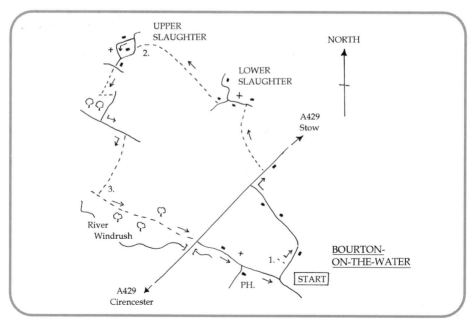

continues up the right-hand side of a hillside field to a gate in the top corner. On the other side of this gate, turn left and follow a wall on the left for just 10 yards to the next gate on the left. Beyond this gate, follow a grassy track downhill for 250 yards to reach a lane. Follow this lane to the right up to a road junction, turn left and follow what is often a fast, busy road – signposted to Bourton – for 300 yards before forking right along a prominent track. Keep on this track to a gate, then continue along the left edges of two fields down into the Windrush Valley. At the far side of the second field, continue along an enclosed track down into the valley bottom to reach a junction with the Windrush Way.

The corn mill at Lower Slaughter

❸ Turn left and follow this right of way as it borders the wooded trackbed of a former railway. In 400 yards, beyond a gate, continue along this path across the right edge of an open field – with the Windrush in the valley on the right. At the far side of the field, pass through a handgate and follow an enclosed path along to the A429. Cross over, and follow the road opposite – Landsdowne – initially on a pavement bordering the Windrush. In 300 yards, immediately past a property called the Mill House, turn right away from the road on a footpath that takes you down to the Windrush. Follow the river downstream for 20 yards to a footbridge, cross the water and turn left to continue alongside the river. On reaching a handgate, follow the left edge of a field – with the river on the left – and, part way across the field, bear half-right away from the Windrush to a gate at the end of a wooden fence. Walk down an enclosed path to join Sherborne Street in Bourton, and turn

left to follow this road back up to the High Street where the Old Manse Hotel is on the right. Walk to the right along the High Street to its junction with Station Road, before turning left back up to the car park entrance.

Place of Interest

Stow-on-the-Wold, just 4 miles north of Bourton-on-the-Water, has been a meeting place from Roman times to the present day. It boasts one of the finest market squares in the country, complete with its market cross, where the final skirmishes of the Civil War took place in 1646. Stow is regarded as a major centre for antiques and fine art galleries outside London but also has a happy blend of tearooms, hotels, pubs and shops, all set within its 17th and 18th century buildings. The Cotswold architecture has been built in mellow honey coloured stone and the area is designated an Area of Outstanding Natural Beauty. Telephone the Tourist Information Centre on 01451 831082 for further information.

Date walk completed:

....

125

delightful walk that encompasses two of the finest villages in the Cotswolds – Stanton and Stanway – where visitors will find examples of definitive Cotswold architecture. There is scarcely a building in Stanton that is not a delight to the eye, whether it be the well-proportioned Perpendicular church, the Court, the manor house or the picture postcard cottages. All are lovingly fashioned from the golden local stone. Stanway is dominated by its fine manor house with its magnificent 17th century gatehouse. From these villages, a stiff climb of over 600 feet up through Lidcombe Wood brings the walk onto the high 'wolds. The view as the path descends back into Stanton at journey's end is quite exceptional, ranging as far afield as the Malvern Hills, the Shropshire Hills and the Brecon Beacons.

The main village street in Stanton climbs the lower slopes of the Cotswolds to reach the **Mount Inn**, a wholly appropriate name given its location on a small knoll. The most popular spot at this Donnington's hostelry is the terraced garden, with its fine views that extend across the village and as far as the distant Welsh Hills. With its exposed stonework, flagstone flooring and grand fireplace, a traditional feel greets patrons of the Mount Inn. As well as the fine Donnington's beers, brewed in nearby Stow-on-the-Wold, the Mount offers all manner of traditional pub fare, ranging from rolls and sandwiches to steak, fish and chicken dishes.

Opening times are 11 am to 3 pm and 6 pm to 11 pm every day.

Telephone: 01386 584316.

Distance: 5 miles

OS Outdoor Leisure 45 The Cotswolds GR 072342

Tracks and footpaths in and around the steep Cotswold escarpment

Starting point: The Mount Inn at Stanton.

How to get there: Stanton lies just ½ mile off of the B4632 (formerly the A46) Broadway to Cheltenham road, 3 miles south of Broadway. As you enter the village, bear left along the main street, a cul-de-sac, which leads up to the Mount. There is roadside parking in the village below the inn.

The Walk

1 From the Mount Inn, head downhill through Stanton to a junction in 300 yards just past the village cross. Turn left and, in 150 yards, where the road bears right, follow the Cotswold Way on the left past some properties to a handgate and marker post on the right. Stay on the Cotswold Way for 1 mile across seven

fields to reach the lane in Stanway – directions are unnecessary with the path being extremely well worn and well signposted. On reaching the lane in Stanway, turn left and continue for 200 yards to the church.

2 Walk past Stanway church and, having passed the impressive gateway to Stanway House, continue to a track on the left signposted as the Cotswold Way. Walk down past a cottage, before keeping along the left-hand grassy path to a wooden gate and an old orchard. Cross this orchard to a handgate and the B4077. Follow the pavement to the left for 600 yards and, on reaching a sharp right-hand bend, walk ahead along a cul-de-sac lane to a fork in 75 yards, and keep left along the path to Stanton and Snowshill. Follow the path ahead that runs along the northern edge of Lidcombe Wood, climbing steeply all the while and ignoring all side tracks. In 600 yards, keep on the path as it bears left and reaches a junction by a small green in the woodland.

3 Turn right immediately before this green and, ignoring all side turns, follow the main track ahead uphill through the woodland, with a stream

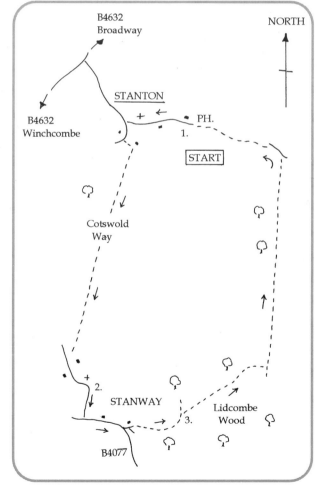

127

over on the right. In ½ mile, pass through an old gateway and leave the woodland. Continue ahead along the hilltop track, with an arable field on the right, for 200 yards to a gate and a junction with a bridleway. Turn left and follow the bridleway across the hilltop for ¾ mile to a gate, parking area and lane. Follow the lane to the left – it becomes an unmetalled track – and keep on the track as it drops down the hillside towards Stanton, ignoring the Cotswold Way that comes in on the left and heads off on the right very early on. In ¾ mile, at the foot of the hill, go through a gate and continue down a sunken track to reach the top of the lane

The village cross in Stanton

in Stanton. Continue ahead for a few yards to the Mount Inn.

Date walk completed:

....

Places of Interest

The **Gloucestershire and Warwickshire Railway**, the 'GWR', is a steam and diesel heritage railway located at Toddington, just a mile or so west along the B4077 from Stanway. Since 1981, volunteers have restored over 10 miles of line, together with platforms, buildings, steam and diesel locomotives and rolling stock. In addition to a scheduled service, the GWR hosts a number of galas and enthusiasts' events throughout the year. Telephone: 01242 621405; website: www.gwsr.com

Snowshill Manor, a National Trust property, lies just a few miles east of Stanton. As well as the manor, there is an 'Arts and Crafts' style garden with terraces and ponds that was laid out in the early 20th century by Charles Paget Wade as a series of outdoor rooms. Now run on organic principles, it has a lively mix of ornaments and architectural features, bright colours and delightful scents, with wonderful views across the Cotswold countryside. Telephone: 01386 852410.